David McClay was the inaugural seni
Archive at the National Library of
works at the University of Edinburg
all eras interesting, the Romantic pe..............................walter
Scott, Lord Byron and Jane Austen, is among his favourites. David
himself doesn't write as many letters as he feels he should.

Praise for Dear Mr Murray

'Attractively arranged, given ample context and a diverting read'
Sunday Telegraph

'An entertaining picture of the day-to-day dealings between author
and publisher over 250 years'　　　　　　*Times Literary Supplement*

'Few, if any, names in publishing are as revered as John Murray . . .
This book, compiled to celebrate the company's 250th anniversary
is just a small sampling of [Murray's] treasure trove . . . Whether
angry, apologetic, wheedling or rude, the fondness and regard in
which the Murrays were held by their correspondents shines
through'　　　　　　　　　　　　　　　　　　　　　　　*Herald*

'A sparkling anthology'　　　　　　　　　　　　*Scots Magazine*

'Writers writing about books has always made for compelling reading. Writers writing about their *own* books in private correspondence
to their publisher tends to produce a particular kind of letter. There
is passion, conviction, fluency, doubt, deference, sometimes frustration and anger, maybe even gratitude. The letters in *Dear Mr Murray*
. . . show these qualities and more . . . McClay has excerpted the
Murray side of correspondence skilfully . . . this collection brings
[Murray's] salad days inexorably to life'　　*Scottish Review of Books*

'As well as allowing us glimpses behind the public faces of some
exalted authors, McClay has paid tribute here to a remarkable line
whose shared name became synonymous with a sense of responsibility
to their company, their authors and literature itself'　　　　*Nation*

50 Albemarle Street by Alan Powers

DEAR
MR
MURRAY

Letters to a
Gentleman Publisher

Selected and introduced by
David McClay

JOHN MURRAY

First published in Great Britain in 2018 by John Murray (Publishers)
An Hachette UK company

This paperback edition published in 2019

1

Foreword copyright © John R. Murray 2018
Copyright in the selection, introduction and editorial matter
© David McClay 2018

A CIP catalogue record for this title is available from the British Library

Paperback ISBN 978-1-47366-270-4
eBook ISBN 978-1-47366-271-1

Design by Georgina Widdrington

Typeset in Bembo Std by Palimpsest Book Production Limited, Falkirk, Stirlingshire

Printed and bound in Great Britain by Clays Ltd, Elcograf S.p.A.

John Murray policy is to use papers that are natural,
renewable and recyclable products and made from wood grown
in sustainable forests. The logging and manufacturing processes are
expected to conform to the environmental regulations of
the country of origin.

John Murray (Publishers)
Carmelite House
50 Victoria Embankment
London EC4Y 0DZ

www.johnmurray.co.uk

To John and Virginia Murray

CONTENTS

CONTENTS

FOREWORD

To be born a Murray was something extraordinary and this dawned on me early on. While I was at boarding school my father used to write letters to me giving me news of what was going on at 50 Albemarle Street, the home and later publishing offices of the Murrays since 1812. These letters quickly made clear that publishing to the Murrays was a lifestyle. I heard of my father exploring parish churches with John Piper and John Betjeman in preparation for their county guides, and visiting Dame Felicitas Corrigan, who was in the enclosed order of Benedictine nuns at Stanbrook Abbey. As a rule he was separated from her by a grille, but on this occasion she was in hospital and he received special dispensation as a lay person to sit beside her bed while discussing the proofs of her book, *In a Great Tradition*, a study of the friendship of her late abbess, Dame Laurentia McLachlan, with Bernard Shaw and Sir Sydney Cockerell. Another letter to me described the excitement when Paddy Leigh Fermor tracked down Byron's slippers in Missolonghi and sent back a tracing of them for my father to check against Byron's boots in our collection. Then there was the evening spent in the drawing room at 50 Albemarle Street with Harold Nicolson and Peter Quennell reading through original Byron letters brought up from the archive, trying to discover what Byron was up to on a certain day in May 1815 that was clearly a vital piece of information required by Harold Nicolson for a book he was writing. These and many other fascinating tidbits reached me by letter and revealed to me at a young age the immediacy of correspondence.

I was to discover over the years that the Murrays were much more than publishers. James Hogg, the 'Ettrick Shepherd', asked John Murray II to find him a wife and Byron asked him to collect from the London docks the body of his illegitimate daughter Allegra who had died in a convent in Italy, and to arrange for her to be buried in Harrow Church. It can only be imagined the problems he must have faced trying to persuade the rector and churchwardens to agree, as Allegra was illegitimate and Byron notorious. They finally consented to her being interred beside the porch. Murray also supplied Byron with magnesia, gunpowder, tooth powders and was even asked to send two English bulldogs to him in Italy. Byron in return sent Murray relics from the battlefield of Waterloo and bones from the battlefield of Morat where, in the fifteenth century, the Swiss defeated the Burgundians. Joanna Baillie, the Scottish-born dramatist, sent him the skin of a Scottish sea monster and Paul Du Chaillu, the African explorer, asked John Murray III to arrange for a gorilla to be stuffed. John Murray III was also a good friend of David Livingstone and among other things planned for Livingstone's daughter to receive music lessons in Paris and organised her pocket money. And John Murray IV taught that extraordinary woman traveller Isabella Bird to ride a tricycle up Albemarle Street. These demands on the Murrays continued after the Second World War when Freya Stark asked John Murray VI to send her a hip-bath to the Hadhramaut by diplomatic bag, and Noni Jabavu, the first Bantu author to be published in English, asked John Murray VII to send her in Africa 'Plush Prune' nail varnish. In these and many other instances the Murrays went well beyond the usual duties of a publisher.

The Murrays' close relationship with their authors was underlined by the choice of godparents for their children. Henry Layard, who discovered Nimrud and Nineveh, was the godfather of John Murray III's younger son, Hallam; Francis Younghusband, who led Lord Curzon's notorious invasion of Tibet in 1904, was my elder sister Joanna's godfather; Freya Stark, the Arabian traveller, was my godmother; Osbert Lancaster, the cartoonist, writer and theatre designer, was my younger sister Freydis's godfather; and the painter John Piper, my brother Hallam's godfather.

Over the seven generations the Murrays emerged as a 'dynasty' and were careful to preserve their correspondence, and by 2006 it consisted of over 500,000 manuscript letters as well as manuscripts of many of their authors' works. It was the largest private publishing archive in the world and covered correspondence with many of the most important people of the time – writers, explorers, scientists, politicians and archaeologists. The correspondence of the Murrays was often forthright but always fair and this was why so many authors wished to be published by them. Jane Austen remarked that John Murray II was 'a rogue of course, but a civil one' and then chose him to publish *Emma*. The Murrays were not always seen to be generous to their authors, but they had a reputation for being excellent publishers and for being able to promote their authors' books through their wide circle of influential contacts. It was John Murray II who persuaded Walter Scott to review *Emma* in the *Quarterly Review* and John Murray IV who, at the request of Schliemann, persuaded Gladstone – against his better judgement – to write a preface to his *Mycenae*.

This was the background that inspired the idea for this

anthology, *Dear Mr Murray: Letters to a Gentleman Publisher*, but it is only a taster of what can be found in the vast collection of letters now in the John Murray Archive in the National Library of Scotland, and of the pleasure and immediacy to be gained from reading original correspondence.

John Murray VII
London, June 2018

THE SEVEN GENERATIONS OF
JOHN MURRAY

———•———

John Murray I (1737–93)

Born in Edinburgh as a McMurray, he took his friend's advice to drop the 'wild Highland Mac' upon starting his London publishing business. Ambitious and hardworking, he was also, as was typical of the age, hard-drinking. Publishing in many genres and formats, a large number of his successes came from his Edinburgh connections and his medical publications. However, his ambition to publish a book that would appeal to millions remained unfulfilled.

John Murray II (1778–1843)

He moved the family business from London's Fleet Street to Albemarle Street, becoming, in consequence, a gentleman publisher during the Romantic period. He published many poets, none more famous or controversial than Lord Byron, with whom – as a friend and author – he had a remarkable correspondence. However, Murray was essentially an establishment figure, publisher to the Admiralty and founder of the conservative periodical the *Quarterly Review*. Further successes with cookery books and children's history insulated him against the huge losses of the *Representative*, a failed newspaper venture.

John Murray III (1808–92)

His particular interest in science, travel and exploration created a change in the Murray publishing output. His own early travels led to the launch in 1836 of the famous series of *Handbooks for Travellers*, for long the benchmark of such books and imitated by many followers including Baedeker. He also published numerous famous explorers of the age, becoming intimate friends with many of them, including David Livingstone and Isabella Bird. The refutation in his own work, *Scepticism in Geology* (1878), of the scientific and geological theories of two of his most important authors Sir Charles Lyell and Charles Darwin was wisely published anonymously under the pseudonym Verifier.

John Murray IV (1851–1928)

Tensions with his artistic brother, Hallam, led to a family split. A key figure in the publishing profession, he was a founder and afterwards president of the Publishers Association and an important influence behind the Net Book Agreement and the Copyright Act of 1911 which established that copyright arises in the act of creation, not publishing. He began the publishing of the *Letters of Queen Victoria* (1907–32), for which he received a knighthood, and which led to a publicity and legal battle with *The Times* newspaper, which Murray won. His greatest publishing success was unexpected: Axel Munthe's *The Story of San Michele* (1929) sold over a million copies in Britain and was translated into thirty-seven languages.

John 'Jack' Murray V (1884–1967)

A decorated military hero of the First World War, he acquired the publisher Smith, Elder and Company in 1917, which brought to Murray's many valuable copyrights, including those of polar explorers and notable works of fiction, as well as the literary journal, the *Cornhill Magazine*. Murray was knighted in 1932 following the successful publication of the ninth and final volume of *Letters of Queen Victoria*. He was the last editor of the long-running journal, and mainstay of the company, the *Quarterly Review*.

John 'Jock' Murray VI (1909–93)

The nephew of John Murray V reinvigorated the company and reignited the literary and social spark of John Murray II. He was described by his Magdalen College fellow student, bestselling author and friend John Betjeman as 'Very shy & saintly & high minded & unshockable & shrewd & kind & conscientious & clever'. In 1975 he received a CBE for services to literature. His tenure was particularly associated with extensive collecting, publication and expert promotion relating to the life, letters and poetry of Lord Byron.

John Murray VII (1941–)

Current head of the Murray family, who, in 2002, after 234 years of distinguished independence, made the difficult decision to sell the business. Despite the lack of family involvement, Murray's has continued, as an imprint of Hodder & Stoughton, to be responsible for many interesting and popular titles. He also arranged, by sale and donation, the transfer of the unparalleled family and business archives to the National Library of Scotland, thereby ensuring that the history of this remarkable publishing house is available for all to discover, research, enjoy and celebrate.

Dr. Tehyi Hsieh
1468 Comm. Ave.
Brighton, 35. Mass.

AFTER 5 DAYS RETURN TO

His Excellency
Sir John Murray, K.C.V.O., D.S.O.
The Messrs John Murray Company Publishers
50 Albermarle Street
London, W.1. England.

VIA
AIRMAIL

INTRODUCTION

For any business to last 250 years is remarkable. For a publishing business to do so, when almost every venture is a risk, is exceptional. In 2018 the publishing house of John Murray celebrates a quarter-millennial history. When Edinburgh-born John Murray set up in London's Fleet Street in 1768, he would have little expected such longevity to his name and publishing house, and as recently as 2002 the business was still in the founding family's ownership. It was the seventh John Murray who sold the business that year, allowing it to continue to thrive into another century as a successful imprint of John Murray Press, part of Hodder & Stoughton.

Longevity certainly added to the status and fame of Murray's. However, as Sir Bruce Lyttelton Richmond, editor of the *Times Literary Supplement*, pointed out in a dispute with John Murray IV in 1920: 'it is true that people who care greatly for literature . . . do not as a rule notice or care by whom a book is published.' While Murray's authors' names are likely to carry greater resonance than those of the company's owners, their reputation and recognition have often been high. The explorer Paul Belloni Du Chaillu could write to John Murray III from New York in 1871 that 'everybody who is not a donkey knows the name of John Murray here, for your father and your publications have gone all over the world where the English language is spoken.' Such was the fame of the Murrays that Arthur W. Beall could address his 1932 letter from Ontario, Canada, to 'John Murray, The World-wide famous Book & Publishing House, London, England' and be confident that it would arrive.

Another correspondent from Fukushima, Japan, addressed a 1978 airmail letter 'To kind English post-office clerks. Messrs John Murray, London, ENGLAND (I do not know the correct address of this company. It is a publishing company that published a lot of books of Sherlock Holmes, such as "The Annotated Sherlock Holmes", "The Complete Sherlock Holmes, Short Stories", "The Complete Sherlock Holmes, Long Stories." Please be kind enough to send this letter there.)' The letter arrived safely and promptly, unlike other correspond-ence that barely made it at all. Two singed and blackened letters to Murray's were stamped 'SALVAGED MAIL AIRCRAFT CRASH SINGAPORE 13.3.1954'.

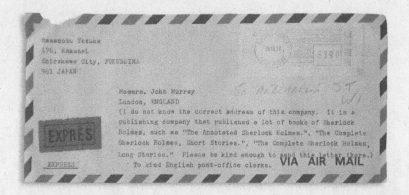

Other correspondence suffered remarkable postage delay, for example a book catalogue received in 1975 had been sent to Karachi, Pakistan, and returned stamped 'TRAPPED IN SUEZ SINCE 1967'.

Consistent across the generations has been the continued reliance on correspondence in conducting business. Letters flowed to and from Murray's authors – including both the prospective and the rejected – customers and readers, as well as people from every part of the publication process, encompassing literary readers, editors, translators, artists, engravers, printers, binders, lawyers, agents, booksellers and film companies. They reveal not only the story of some of the most interesting and influential books in history, but also the remarkable friendships that were built up – as well as occasional animosities.

When the biographer Samuel Smiles was being encouraged to undertake a biography of John Murray II, his son wrote to Smiles: 'I may venture to assure you that the materials for it are copious and most interesting; if you undertook it, it would be the pleasure and duty of my son and myself to aid and assist you in every way in our power.' Even with the help of several Murray family members Smiles found the task of working through such a large collection daunting, spending twelve years on what his granddaughter recalled him describing as 'a long and tedious business' from which he 'caught a bad cold searching through those germy archives'. However, his subsequent biography, *A Publisher and his Friends: Memoir and correspondence of the late John Murray, with an account of the origin and progress of the house, 1768–1843* (1891), made extensive use of the archive and showed the importance of letters to Murray's in telling their publishing story.

The following selection of letters to the first six Murrays, while covering a wide range of authors, genres and themes, is by no means intended to be comprehensive, but it provides a flavour of the rich history and archives of one of the most famous names in publishing.

The Murrays established and maintained a reputation as gentlemen publishers, whose interest in the books they were publishing was matched by their concern to deal with their authors fairly; however their sound understanding of business and knowledge of the book trade itself must never be overlooked.

The first John Murray appreciated the importance of a bestseller to balance the books. In 1775 he asked the historian John Whitaker: 'Commend me . . . to a saleable work such as *Pilgrim's Progress* or *Robinson Crusoe* that will please the million. What signifies a learned and ingenious book to me when there are not learned and ingenious men enough to buy it.' In 1783 he suggested to Whitaker that for 'a saleable work it should be addressed to the mob of readers, to literary amateurs, & to smatterers in taste . . . to slender as well as profound capacities: if you are able to entertain the ladies your business is done.'

The precarious nature of publishing profitably was echoed by John Murray III, who wrote in 1880: 'A book before it is published is like a lottery ticket, it may turn out a blank or a prize.' The Murrays enjoyed a number of prizes, bestsellers to please the mob and million, though these were irregular and difficult to predict. They included the poetry of Lord Byron and John Betjeman, works of exploration and travel from the likes of David Livingstone and Patrick Leigh Fermor, as well as self-help, children's and cookery books, with classical diction-aries, travel guidebooks, school textbooks, periodicals and Navy Lists also bringing essential profits. Early twentieth-century international bestsellers, including P. C. Wren's *Beau Geste* (1924) and Axel Munthe's *The Story of San Michele* (1929), also brought interest for film adaptation, with American companies desperate to purchase the rights.

While the Murrays had their fair share of bestsellers, such works were easily outnumbered by those that barely made a profit. Many even made a loss. John Murray II lamented in the 1820s that 'woeful experience convinces me that not more than one publication in fifty has a sale sufficient to defray its expenses.' This concern was mirrored by his grandson a century later, when he wrote that 'It was reckoned that out of all the books published at the time not more than one in fifty paid its expenses.' John Murray III had a partial explanation for the vagaries of the bookselling market, writing to his friend and author William Gladstone in the late 1840s: 'It must be borne in mind that books are a luxury. When a time of distress comes, the first expense to be curtailed is the purchase of books. That is done (without any outward display of economy) rather than laying down a carriage or dismissing servants.'

While a publisher might struggle to balance the books, authors, even successful ones, also found it difficult to make a living. The prolific and profitable author Samuel Smiles advised his son Willie, who was proposing to write a social history of

England: 'Literature is not to be pursued as a profession for a good living cannot – except in rare cases – be made out of it; but it is very pleasant as an adjunct and as an amusement. I merely fill in idle moments with it.'

Books did not remain exclusive and expensive items. As the nineteenth century progressed a growing literary class had increasing access to writing of quality. With an improving economy, technological developments in all aspects of book production and the expansion of libraries, published works became more widely affordable and accessible. Each Murray generation not only coped, but thrived, on the demands and expectations of this burgeoning readership. At one time or another, the Murrays published in practically every format and genre, often innovating, but always maintaining their reputation and tradition for producing high-quality and influential works.

One prized Murray author who recognised the inherent financial tension in the publisher–author relationship was Lord Byron. In writing to his financial adviser Douglas Kinnaird, on 14 July 1821, he stated: 'I believe M. to be a good man with a personal regard for me. But a bargain is in its very essence a hostile transaction . . . do not all men try to abate the price of all they buy? I contend that a bargain even between brethren – is a declaration of war. Now this must be much more so in a man like M. whose business is nothing but perpetual specu-lation on what will or will not succeed.' Despite these natural tensions John Murray II was considered one of the first gentlemen in the trade, with Scottish journalist William Jerdan in his *Autobiography* (1853) full of praise: 'Murray was a character, and a character in which the estimable qualities predominated far above the questionable infirmities of our human nature. He was a prince and a gentleman among publishers, and the least of a huckstering tradesman I almost ever knew in that or any other trade.' Fellow publisher William Blackwood wrote to him admiringly that 'you have the happiness of making it a liberal profession, and not a mere business of pence.'

John Murray II's growing reputation had been enhanced by moving, in 1812, from Fleet Street to 50 Albemarle Street in London's fashionable West End. There Murray established himself as a patron of literature. As he boastfully wrote to his half-brother Archie in 1813: 'I have lately ventured on the bold step of quitting the old establishment to which I have been so long attached, and have moved to one of the best, in every respect, that is known in my business, where I have succeeded in a manner the most complete and flattering. My house is excellent; and I transact all the departments of my business in an elegant library, which my drawing-room becomes during the morning; and there I am in the habit of seeing persons of the highest rank in literature and talent, such as [George] Canning, [John Hookham] Frere, [James] Mackintosh, [Robert] Southey, [Thomas] Campbell, Walter Scott, Madame de Stael, [William] Gifford, [John Wilson] Croker, [John] Barrow, Lord Byron, and others; thus leading the most delightful life, with means of prosecuting my business with the highest honour and emolument.'

Novelist Anna Eliza Bray recalled: 'At Mr Murray's frequent parties we met several persons of eminence in the world of art and literature. John Murray (King John we used to call him, for his munificence and the manner in which he took the lead of all the publishers in London) showed a great deal of taste and spirit concerning his authors . . . The wit of Murray, combined with his vivacity and his hospitality, caused his society to be eagerly sought, and many were anxious to be on such terms with him as to be admitted to the delightful dinner-parties he gave to so intellectual a circle.'

Generation by generation the authors changed, but always

a Murray remained at the centre of a glittering literary nexus at No. 50. Scientists talked to politicians, poets met critics, cookery writers consulted explorers. The circle of John 'Jock' Murray VI (1909–93) was arguably as varied and interesting as that of any previous age, Osbert Lancaster, Freya Stark and John Betjeman mirroring that of Murray II's Thomas Phillips, Maria Graham and Lord Byron. Admiration for the special nature of the Murray relationship persisted. Travel writer Dervla Murphy could write as recently as 1991 that 'I reckon the Murray/Murphy relationship is by now an anachronism – sad . . . It appalled me to hear so many authors talking about their publishers as though they were <u>enemies</u>. How can writers function in such an atmosphere?'

Numerous examples of the Murrays' gentlemanly behaviour may be found throughout each generation. John Murray I, for instance, was repeatedly praised by his friend, literary adviser and author Gilbert Stuart when recommending him to Sir David Dalrymple, Lord Hailes, as a publisher for his history, *Annals of Scotland* (1776–9). Stuart wrote in 1775: 'Mr Murray of Fleet Street . . . is exceedingly active & intelligent in his profession, & of great integrity. And I am certain would manage your book with address & skill'; then: 'I cannot but say, to his praise, that I have found him in a multiplicity of transactions, attentive & intelligent beyond what I could have expected from a bookseller.'

Walter Scott, writing on 30 October 1828 to his son-in-law John Gibson Lockhart, who was to produce an abridgement of his *Life of Napoleon* (1827), played on Murray II's nickname of the 'emperor of the west': 'By all means do what the Emperor asks. He is what the Emperor Napoleon was not, much a gentleman, and knowing our footing in all things.' John Murray III was royally praised by Du Chaillu, who in 1862 wrote: 'How kind Mr Murray the king of publishers has been to me.'

Following John Murray II's death in 1843 it was widely published that 'Mr Murray's career as a publisher is one continued history of princely payments. His copyrights were secured at the most extravagant prices – for he never haggled about the sum if he wanted the work.'

Authors and printers alike admired John Murray III. As editor of the *Quarterly Review* (1867–93), and compiler of extensively illustrated dictionaries and encyclopedias, Sir William 'Dictionary' Smith was a key figure at Murray's in the late nineteenth century. According to John Murray IV his books, among them his dictionaries of the Bible, Greek and Roman Antiquities, Christian Biography, Christian Antiquities, Latin dictionaries and Ancient Atlas, required an outlay by Murray III of almost £150,000, a colossal sum at the time. They were lucrative and challenging works for the printer to produce, and when problems arose and Murray III threatened to remove Smith's titles to another printer, Clowes responded with the following letter.

George Clowes to John Murray III, Stamford Street, London, 29 January 1866

My Dear Sir

Before sending the plates of Dr Smith's Smaller Latin Dictionary to Albemarle S. I am requested by my brother, son & nephew to ask you kindly to reconsider your decision and to offer either to deduct from our Christmas account the amount for printing it viz £127, or to print the next edition of 5,000 copies without charge, producing the very best impression from the plates which with strict vigilance & care is possible.

In addition to the engagement of an extra overseer at a

high salary to watch the impressions, as I emphasised to you, and for whose ability as the best judge of work in the trade Mr Cooper, the wood engraver, can vouch, we have just incurred an expenditure of more than £2,000 in 3 new machines and additional presses to meet your requirements, and place us above any temporary pressure, although in the general way they may not be necessary.

I can assure you that I have for more than 30 years attended to your interests as a labour of love, in addition to my full acknowledgement of the very valuable assistance your house renders to the great difficulty of working a large establishment and keeping it in active operation. At the same time I would add without presumption or any vain boasting, that I feel confident no other firm in the world could or would strive more earnestly or zealously, or make a more profuse expenditure in time and machinery, to enable you to carry on your important undertakings with that great facility which these extensive resources place at your command.

I am, My Dear Sir
Always yours sincerely and obliged
George Clowes

Smith's letter of condolence to the Murray family on the death of Murray III told of the admiration and friendship they shared: 'I have known most of the distinguished men during the last two generations, but I know no one who was so universally liked and looked up to and respected in all classes of society, and whose death will be more sincerely regretted. Of my own personal loss I dare hardly think. I have lost my oldest and best friend. I have lived with him in the most intimate friendship for nearly fifty years without one jarring note; and the longer I have known him, the more I have respected, loved and admired him. I have always received from him the most signal marks of confidence, kindness and generosity, and I feel that his death will darken my declining years.' Smith died the following year.

When trying to track down a copy of a book he had published years earlier, the traveller William Edwards was repeating the, often forlorn, wishes of countless authors before and after him. In this case he was fortunate that his sixty-year-old book had been published by Murray's.

William Henry Edwards to John Murray IV, Coalburgh, West Virginia, USA, 16 September 1907

Dear Sir

I wish to get twenty or less copies of my 'Voyage up the River Amazon', published by your house in 1847, if the book is still to be had. Please kindly inform me as to this last, and what the cost of the twenty or less copies will be, and I will send a Postal Order forthwith.

I was in London in 1848, and saw the then Mr Murray several times. He did me the honor of inviting me to dinner on one occasion.

Yours very respectfully
Wm H. Edwards

On 30 October 1909 Murray replied: 'It was a surprise and pleasure to me to receive your letter . . . for your name has been familiar to me during the 35 years of my business life here . . . yes your book is still kept in stock . . . I hope you will accept the 20 copies I send today as a present from my father and myself . . . [we're] glad to hear of the author after so long an interval.' To which Edwards replied: 'Your letter of

30th ult. reached me on the 11th and the four packages of books followed next day, all in good condition. I am exceedingly obliged to your brother and yourself for this handsome gift. It enables me to provide each of my children a copy of the book I wrote at 24 years of age. One immediate result of that book was to send Wallace and Bates to the Amazon.'

Despite the Murrays' natural inclinations towards generosity and gentlemanly behaviour, misunderstandings and disputes inevitably occurred. As John Murray IV noted in his essay 'Darwin and his Publisher' in *Science Progress* (1909): 'The relations between authors and publishers have long formed the subject of satire and ridicule in prose and verse.'

Disputes over copyright payments, share of profits and production expenses might easily cause tensions in the author–publisher relationship and quarrels might arise from misunderstandings of the complexities of the publishing process since almost every stage of book production can be problematic. As the American writer and essayist Mary Abigail Dodge wrote in *A Battle of the Books* (1870): 'The elder John Murray, one of the most honorable and generous of publishers, used to say, that an author who thoroughly understood all the intricacies and expenses of issuing a book from the press, and properly launching it into the hands of the public, was as rare a prize to find as a phoenix or a unicorn.'

The selection process for this anthology has been a considerable challenge, such is the number and quality of letters available. Preference has been given to those that contain a mixture of publishing and personal content. This may be the case with even the briefest, such as the following letter from the future Prime Minister William Gladstone.

William Ewart Gladstone to John Murray III, Carlton Gardens, London, 2 July 1850

¼ to 12 PM.

My dear Sir

I send herewith some MS of the speech for the printer to begin upon.

You will grieve to learn that Sir Robert Peel is dead –

within the last half hour – i.e. at a quarter past eleven. A great man is gone from among us, & a broad & deep void, not easily to be filled, remains.

I am always
Sincerely yours
W. Gladstone

Some letters were simply too long to justify inclusion. A few had handwriting that was nearly unreadable. This isn't just a challenge to the modern editor: John Murray IV in an article for the popular monthly magazine *Good Words* noted that: 'Dean Stanley's bad handwriting is a matter of common notoriety . . . Once he wrote to my father a letter on an important matter, but there were some passages in it which, in spite of every effort, proved indecipherable. My father was consequently compelled to underline these sentences and to return the letter, with a request that they might be re-written. In due course the Dean replied: "If you cannot read my writing, I am sure I cannot do so; but I think I meant to say," so and so, and the sentence was rewritten in a form scarcely more legible than before.'

Murray's published important and influential works on politics, philosophy, religion and science. Other titles – travel, biography, history, drama, poetry or novels – primarily aimed to entertain. But whatever the genre of literature involved, all these works required the involvement of a publisher to bring the book before an audience. As the following selection of letters makes clear, this was rarely done without a lot of hard work, the occasional quarrel, and a network of people besides the author and publisher who left behind a remarkable body of correspondence.

Wherever possible, original abbreviations, punctuation, variant spellings and errors have been retained. However, as this book is intended for the general reader, minor adjustments have been made where necessary to ensure that the original letters make sense.

On 7 April 1815 the two greatest writers of the age, Sir Walter
Scott and Lord Byron (shown on the right), met at John Murray's
premises at 50 Albemarle Street. This later reconstruction also
includes (from left to right) Isaac D'Israeli, John Murray II,
Sir John Barrow, George Canning and William Gifford.

1

'Your goodness and readiness
to oblige your friends'
Entertaining

John Murray I published *An Essay on Nothing. A discourse delivered in a society* (1776) by his friend Hugo Arnot, the lawyer, historian and campaigner, and co-published, with William Creech, his *History of Edinburgh* (1779). Arnot took advantage of Murray's wide-ranging network of suppliers of fine alcoholic drinks.

Hugo Arnot to John Murray I, Edinburgh, 26 January 1775

Dear Sir

Since I am so far lucky as to have you in my debt for a letter, I shall not say that I never write you except to plague you with commissions, yet I will freely confess that I would not have written you just now, was it not to beg the favour of you to buy me a hogshead of the best porter & send it down by the first ship. I am so confident of your goodness & readiness to oblige your friends, that I presume you will not think an apologie necessary for giving you the trouble. I assure you nothing will make me happier than your drinking a mug of it with me, & taking a slice of beef rump some evening next summer. I had the pleasure of dining lately Miss Macmurray with her & Mrs Finlay, who were then very well as was your niece Katie who also honoured us with her company – I had a letter a few weeks since from our friend David Ross who is very fond of Dublin. He declares it to be the best & cheapest place for good living he ever saw & talks of fixing his standard there; if that were the case and I had some cash to spare, I should like much to accompany you in a trip to Dublin – Wattie Ross has been rearing a fairy land near the Water of Leith, and the consequence of that or of something else, is that his house in Lady Stairs Close & some other houses belonging to him are advertised for sale –

Ask me not about the law, I had a fever in the beginning of winter which prevented my attendance. Blessed is he that expecteth nothing, for he will not be mortified by his disappointment. I thank God I can live at present tho it should not bring salt to my children's porridge – but when they are grown up, the affair will be more serious –

If you will send me a pound or two of currie powder (an East Indian powder for dressing fish, chickens &c) it will be adding to other favours – You will draw on me the amount payable to your sister or anybody you please. My wife is nursing & drinks a devilish quantity of porter, we are quite run out, & drouth is very impatient –

We are all very well, Mrs Arnot joins me in best wishes & compliments to you & Mrs Murray.

I am, Dear Sir

Yours very sincerely

Hugo Arnot

Untoward events might sometimes occur at social occasions in the literary world, and following an embarrassing dinner with Murray, William Makepeace Thackeray felt the need to apologise.

William Makepeace Thackeray to John Murray II, Great Coram Street, London, 24 January 1840

Sir

I am sorry to recall to your memory a certain dinner at which I met you about a fortnight since, but I have only heard this evening the particulars of this unfortunate affair. I am bound to offer you the best apologies I can make for my conduct upon the occasion.

My friend Fraser told me (in the strongest possible terms) his opinion of my behaviour at his house, but he gave no particulars, and I confess to you, so entirely had I forgotten every circumstance that had taken place, that I did not until tonight know, how or to whom I had acted wrongly. Mr Jerden, whom I have just seen, informed me of the circumstances and I am obliged − with a very great deal of shame and contrition I assure you − to express my sorrow for what took place. I do not know that I was ever the actor in such a scene before, & can only attribute my behaviour to sickness under which I was then labouring, and by which a not extraordinary quantity of wine was made to act violently upon a disordered stomach.

It must pain you I am sure to be obliged to recur to a subject so disagreeable, but my duty was clear: to apologize to you for what had happened, & to beg you to believe that I never would, in my sober senses, have offered an insult or addressed a slighting word to a gentleman of your age and character.

I am, Sir, your very humble servant
W. M. Thackeray

Author George Borrow acquired an appreciation of different alcoholic drinks during his travels in Spain. He wrote to Murray on 22 February 1842: 'I spent a day last week with our friend Dawson Turner at Yarmouth – what capital port he keeps. He gave me some twenty years old and of nearly the finest flavour that I ever tasted. There are few better things than old books, old pictures and old port, and he seems to have plenty of all three.' A subsequent letter complained of printing delays and offered a toast to his health.

George Borrow to John Murray II, Oulton Hall, Lowestoft, Suffolk, 4 July 1842

My Dear Sir

As I suppose that by this time you have received the balance which I can see to be remitted to London a week ago, I herewith send the account which I will promise you to receipt and then return.

I have received a letter from Mr Woodfall in which he informs me that the work is at a standstill for want of paper, giving me at the same time to understand that it is intentionally delayed – you are aware that when I had last the pleasure of seeing you it was agreed that the book should be brought out on the first of October, which as everyone is aware is the best time in the year for publishing and at which time a great many of my friends expect to see it – Now I do not wish them to be disappointed, more especially as I have frequently assured them since my return from London that there was no doubt of its appearance at that time. I therefore must beg an immediate answer to the question – why this delay? I have been expecting to hear from you for some days past – Mr W. tells me that the state of the trade is wretched. Well and good! But you yourself told me so two months ago, when you wrote requesting that I would give you the preference, provided I had not made arrangements with other publishers. Between ourselves, my dear friend, I wish the state of the trade were ten times worse than it is, and then things would find their true level, and an original work would be properly appreciated, and a set of people who have no pretensions to write, having nothing to communicate but tea-table twaddle, could no longer be palmed off upon the public as mighty lions and lionesses – but to the question, what are your intentions with respect to The Bible in Spain? I am a frank man, and frankness never offends me. Has anybody put you out of conceit with the book? There is no lack of critics, especially in your neighbourhood. Tell me frankly, and I will drink your health in Rommany –

Or, would the appearance of The Bible on the first of October interfere with the avatar, first or second, of some very lion or divinity, to whom George Borrow, who is neither, must, of course, give place? Be frank with me, my dear sir, and I will drink your health in Rommany and Madeira.

In case of either of the above possibilities being the fact, allow me to assure you that I am quite willing to release you from your share of the agreement into which we entered. At the same time, I do not intend to let the work fall to the ground, as it has been promised to the public. Unless you go on with it, I shall remit Woodfall the necessary money for the purchase of paper, and when it is ready offer it to the world. If it be but allowed fair play, I have no doubt of its success. It is an original book, on an original subject.

Tomorrow, July 5, I am thirty-nine – have the kindness to

drink my health in Madeira. With kind remembrances to Mr Murray,
    I remain
    My Dear Sir
    Ever most sincerely yours
    George Borrow

Following the death of John Murray II, the next three Murray generations entertained in a less lively style. Herman Melville wrote in 1849 of a party at No. 50 where after the ladies had withdrawn 'the three decanters, port, sherry and claret, were kept going the rounds with great regularity.' However, he found the company dull, especially the writer and *Quarterly Review* editor John Gibson Lockhart, whom he described as being 'full of himself, and expected great homage; knowing him to be a through-going Tory and fish-blooded churchman and conservative . . . I refrained from playing the snob to him like the rest, and the consequence was he grinned at me his ghastly smiles.'

Biographer Samuel Smiles attended Murray's gatherings for most of the second half of the nineteenth century. Initially he was pleased to be with 'a small but brilliant lot', but eventually he complained that among the regular attenders 'some of them are getting fatter and duller from year to year' and that Dr William 'Dictionary' Smith was 'dogmatic and bumptious as usual'.

It was Jock Murray who restored the best drinking and entertaining traditions of Murray II, one appreciative recipient being the poet John Betjeman who often enjoyed a supply of festive alcoholic drinks. Following the publication of *A Few Late Chrysanthemums*, he sent this appreciative note.

John Betjeman to John Murray VI, The Mead, Wantage, Berkshire,
31 December 1954

My Dear Jock

I must first write to thank you for your handsome
present of that bottle of bubbly, old boy. You are a kind old
publisher. We drank it as an <u>apéritif</u> with John Edward
Bowle and his mother, Powlie, Patrick Balfour, Archbishop
and Gervase Matthew before the Boxing Day Luncheon.

I was most surprised at the chorus of praises in the
Sunday papers, it looked as though I had fixed it.

If you are reprinting, please look at the space between
stanzas. I have not a copy of the book here but from what I
remember, the spaces between stanzas are most unnecessarily
unequal in very many places.

Love to you all from

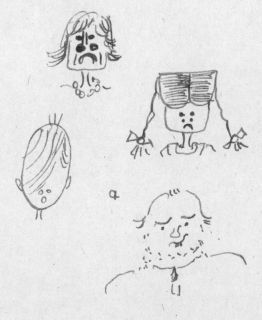

To celebrate Betjeman's knighthood, dinner at the private members club White's was preceded by drinks at No. 50. He wrote to Jock the day after, on 29 July 1969: 'What a jolly evening, Monday night & ta ever so much for making the opening so cheerful at No. 50. Didn't they get gloriously drunk?' It is not known what occasion prompted the following appreciative letter.

John Betjeman to John Murray VI, 23 September 1977

Dear Jock

That was a lovely party last night and it was a joy to see the whole house of Murray on its first floor and to talk to old friends who were all looking more beautiful with the years and more attractive than ever to

Yours ever

J. B.

A New System of Domestic Cookery
Maria Rundell

———◆———

A fter the death of her husband, Maria Rundell began
collecting recipes, household management tips and herbal
remedies for her three married daughters. She also sent a copy
to John Murray II, a family friend, who published them
anonymously as *A New System of Domestic Cookery* (1805). It
proved to be one of the most successful nineteenth-century
cookery books, which by 1841 was on its sixty-fifth edition
and had sold 245,000 copies. It was also one of Murray II's
most valuable copyrights, being used, along with his quarter
share in Walter Scott's *Marmion* (1808) and the *Quarterly Review*,
as surety on his mortgage on 50 Albemarle Street.

While writing to congratulate Murray on his recent
marriage, she could not refrain from complaining bitterly about
the printing errors in the second edition.

Maria Rundell to John Murray II, 28 March 1807

Dear Sir

My last congratulations were premature, accept them now
they are better timed; and with them my sincere good
wishes that the late event may be productive of everything
that can make yourself & Mrs Murray happy, to whom with
Miss M we beg to state. I scarce can forgive your surprise,

that it should promise felicity which you formerly doubted the existence of. It is really well for you that Mrs Murray reclaimed you in time, for if you had nurtured up such ideas a few years longer, you would have been possessed of such bachelor peculiarities, that she may not have ventured to encounter them.

You will I hope forgive my entering on business, in a sheet that ought to have been devoted only to the gayer subject of nuptial celebration, but as the expectation of this event has I regret had some effect on our vulgar publication, we may be forgiven in now calling for the sober attentions of the married man, which the lover could not accord.

In sober English, my good friend, the second edition of D. C. has been miserably prepared for the press. Whoever pretended to correct it has greatly failed; when he saw two receipts for the same thing and heard that they were sent at different times, lest they might have been forgotten, and that I requested a duplicate might not be inserted, he was certainly very remiss in not complying. He has made some dreadful blunders such as directing rice pudding seeds to be kept in a keg of lime water, which latter was mentioned to preserve eggs in – desiring that the round of a cod might be helped instead of the sound [swim bladder], &cc.

If you recollect I told you I had hurried myself greatly even to the serious neglect of my Beckenham concerns to get ready the second edition; but I still hoped it would be put into so careful a hand to arrange, and correct my defi-ciencies, that I should not, or you either feel ashamed of the work; yet upon my word I am quite shocked at the blunders that are crept into it, when it ought to have appeared in better garb – I am seriously afraid this second edition will injure the reputation of the third. Would it not be prudent to suppress it entirely, if no errata can be entered in the present set? You mention that the book is too large, but the person who recommended entering poultry, plates, bills of fare, &c led us into that error, and I am of opinion that the animals [two plates of animals and two pages of letterpress with the various 'cuts' indicated], carving and dinner sets may add to the usefulness of the work.

If anything occurs to you that can be with propriety lopped off, we will expunge and cut away; the sheets I have by me I now send, I have taken several receipts wholly away, and have only written others to be better arranged, as that was another defect.

I don't believe Harriet's watch will come down so soon; as you may want the remaining sheets, preliminary instructions &c, will it not be best to send me down by mail those parts, which I mentioned to Mr Clark to send to my son to forward?

I and my daughters think ourselves much obliged by the books you so kindly forwarded to us; they have much amused us, and for them pray accept our best thanks. I beg you will not be so liberal of the cookery; good eating will be too prevalent. Mrs Strong is dispersing some of hers where most likely to spread the sale – and expressed concern that you would otherwise be a loser by your bounty, by which however she was much indebted, and desired her best thanks. She is now in great affliction, her elder boy being very dangerously ill.

Pray my good friend write by the papers, and tell me what can be done to remedy the blunders. I feel quite wretched, who would have thought that such mistakes should arise! Had I not felt assured that any of mine would have been corrected, I would have desired some friend in town to do them, but besides mine there are many omissions of the <u>correctors</u>, and several things tho small that have been put in – for instance parsley <u>leaves</u>, instead of parsley &c and two receipts wholly omitted which I have sent now, and which were in the first edition.

I hope the errors of this second are done away, and heartily wish a good sale to them – and do not think I shall ever have courage to look at them again.

You will be so good to remember that you promised my account when you should come from Scotland last year; I shall be much in debt to you for it, by the next parcel. You will recollect the 3 works you kindly took charge of – Frederick, Hunter and the anatomy –

We are beginning to talk of our future journey, and are not without expectation of enjoying it as much as that we had down from town. We had a great disappointment lately by the burning down of Mr [Thomas] Johnes fine house at Hafod, which will deprive us of a great pleasure.

You must have heard of a translation he made from Froissart for which Mr White has given him £3,000 it is here said. He is going to rebuild the house, but can never replace the many curious books and other things which money cannot purchase, the loss was £140,000 and 30 only insured.

We are impatiently waiting to hear of F.

Once more let me request that some measure may be immediately taken with all the second edition which you have by you.

I am, Dear Sir

Your obliged friend

Maria Eliza Rundell

Mrs Rundell had originally donated the copyright of the work to Murray. In return, Murray made regular gifts of valuable books to her and her family, which she felt was too generous. She wrote to Murray on 22 May 1807: 'Sir, you must stop your generous hand, for whatever pleasure the works you are so good to send, afford us, we cannot think of putting you to so much trouble.' With her book's unexpected success Murray thought it only fair to share some of the profits, so he made her a gift of £150, prompting this grateful response.

Maria Rundell to John Murray II, Edinburgh, 17 September 1808

My Dear Sir

Your very handsome and most unexpected present I have just received; I can truly say I never had the smallest idea of any return for what I considered, & which really was a free gift to one whom I had long regarded as my friend.

If in truth you have found my little work productive so far above your expectations, as to render your very obliging enclosure a satisfaction to your own feelings, I will not affront your noble sentiment by returning it – although your persuasion of its being honourable to my poor abilities, is really necessary to make me believe I do not err in accepting it –

I beg to return you my best acknowledgements, My Dear Sir, and to assure you of what I however hope you do not doubt, that I am your obliged friend & obedient servant

Maria Eliza Rundell

In the preface to the 1810 edition Mrs Rundell expressly stated that she would receive no further emolument for the work.

However, complaints over the printing and tension over the profits persisted. In 1814 Mrs Rundell accused Murray of neglecting the book and of hindering its sale, prompting Murray to write to his wife that 'her conceit surpasses anything'. In 1821 their publishing relationship had deteriorated further and she offered a revised version of the book to the publisher Longman. Murray's legal adviser obtained an injunction, and with concerns for the mounting legal fees and both Murray's and Longman's inability to publish the work, they eventually settled, signing an agreement on 1 February 1823 whereby Murray confirmed his publishing rights and Mrs Rundell received a substantial settlement of 2,000 guineas (£2,100).

3

'The greatest of all works'
Quarterly Review

———◆———

Arguably Murray's greatest single publishing achievement was the *Quarterly Review*, probably the most influential quarterly of the nineteenth century. With substantial articles on political, scientific, exploration and literary topics, it kept the reader well informed for a relatively modest price. Established in 1809 as a Tory counterblast against the Whiggish *Edinburgh Review*, its founding editor was William Gifford. Walter Scott was a key figure in the creation and editorial direction of the review, contributing dozens of articles, and between 1825 and 1853 his son-in-law John Gibson Lockhart was the journal's editor. This affordable and respected periodical remained in print until 1967 and was responsible for generations of lengthy and often influential articles on a wide range of literary, political and scientific issues.

→→→←←←

Glaswegian Thomas Campbell's sentimental poem *Gertrude of Wyoming* (1809), on the subject of a massacre and torture of American patriots at the Battle of Wyoming, was reviewed anonymously by his friend Walter Scott in the second issue of the *Quarterly Review* after Murray had sent him a copy. Although critical of Campbell's excessively polished style, the review was generally positive and dealt mildly with the poem's unpatriotic depiction of the controversial actions of British loyalists, which Campbell appreciated.

THE

QUARTERLY REVIEW.

MAY, 1809.

ART. I. *Gertrude of Wyoming, a Pensylvanian Tale, and other Poems.* By Thomas Campbell, Author of the Pleasures of Hope, &c. 4to. pp. 130. London, Longman. 1809.

WE open this volume with no ordinary impression of the delicacy and importance of the task which it imposes on us, and the difficulty of discharging it at once with justice to the author and to that public at whose bar we as well as Mr. Campbell must be considered to stand. It is not our least embarrassment that in some respects Mr. Campbell may be considered as his own rival; and in aspiring to extensive popularity has certainly no impediment to encounter more formidable than the extent of his own reputation. To decide on the merit of Gertrude of Wyoming as the work of a poet hitherto undistinguished, would

Thomas Campbell to John Murray II, 2 June 1809

My Dear Murray

I received the review, for which I thank you – and beg leave through you to express my best acknowledgments to the unknown reviewer – I do not by this mean to say that I think every one of his censures just. On the contrary, if I had an opportunity of personal conference with so candid & sensible a man I think I could in some degree acquit myself of a part of the faults he has found – But altogether I am pleased with his manner and very proud of his approbation – He reviews like a gentleman, a Christian & a scholar –

To descend to a less important business, will you have the goodness to send to No. 14 Craven Street Strand for two collections of songs – Riston & Johnson – These have been waiting for Whyte's agent, a Mister Walker, some attorney in Lambeth, to receive some time ago but he never received my letter – I troubled you lately with a list of all Whyte's demands the few volumes [missing] amounting to some 10/6 I shall be much obliged to you to settle for – or give him an order for the books [missing] on Manners & Millar [missing] will get them on my account.

I remain, Dear Murray
Your obliged & sincere friend
T. Campbell

Walter Scott's anonymous *Guy Mannering* (1815) continued his successful invention of the historical novel, begun by *Waverley* (1814), and was reviewed in the *Quarterly Review* by John Wilson Croker, to the disappointment of Scott's friend James Hogg, a literary shepherd, who was trying to make his name as a writer of essays, reviews, short stories, poetry, as well as a novel. Hogg's limited commercial success at this time and his reliance on Scott and others as literary patrons inclined him to defend Scott vigorously and to despise London-based reviews, which he saw as disparaging Scottish literary efforts.

James Hogg to John Murray II, Edinburgh, 31 March 1815

Dear Sir

Are you taken with the <u>pet</u> likewise that you so long neglect to answer a poet's letter? If you are I think you might tell me frankly as usual. I have nothing of consequence to tell you for there are no literary news here of much importance save what the Quarterly has created and what the Edin is just about to create. The Lord of the Isles is in the latter and seems meant as a favourable review; in my opinion however it is <u>scarce middling</u> as we Scots folk say. Mr Scott sails for London in the Pilot today and he asked me if I had no word to you or Lord Byron. I take the opportunity of sending you this as a small remembrancer for I wish to know particularly about The Queen's Wake and how many copies remain in your hand. I have had a very pressing proposal for publishing all my poetical works in two neat post octavo vols. but this I will not so much think of nor any literary thing at present, without consulting you. I myself think it is rather too early to do so as yet. I know I will publish something much better than aught I have yet published if I could hit on a right theme but till that time it will haply be as good to keep them separate and let the things sell that will sell. Pray give me fair play in advertising, reviewing &c; some would insinuate to me that you do the contrary. I have got hold of the Quarterly but have not yet got far on with it. The review of Gibbon is certainly a first-rate article as indeed I think all your principal articles are, but O I am grieved to see such an ignorant and absurd review of Mannering so contrary to the feelings of a whole nation for I certainly never saw high and low, rich and poor so unanimous about any book as that. It is one of those

things which render the whole system of reviewing a mere
farce – What a beast he must be who wrote it! By – if ever
I meet with him I'll insult him and abide the consequences.
I think of all the men in Scotland, Scott has been the most
strenuous supporter of the character of your Miscellany as
excellent, and there is an indelicacy in the thing that cannot
be thought of. How I do despise your London critics.
They persuade you to refuse your name to the Pilgrims of
the Sun and pretend to damn Guy Mannering. I'll keep
both the article and your letter on the former subject, as
two natural curiosities for the next century. But I find I am
in too high a key today for writing to a gentleman whom I
sincerely wish to esteem, therefore without more I will
subscribe myself

 Yours very truly
 James Hogg

Murray replied on 10 April that 'our article is not good, & our
praise is by no means adequate, but I suspect that you very
greatly overrate the novel.'

✦ ✦ ✦ ✦ ✦ ✦

Walter Scott sympathetically reviewed Lord Byron's *Childe
Harold's Pilgrimage, Canto III* (1816) and *Canto IV* (1818) but
was still concerned that he might offend the poet, who had
permanently left England in 1816.

Walter Scott to John Murray II, Edinburgh, 10 January 1817

My Dear Sir

 I have this day sent under Croker's cover a review of
Lord Byron's last poems. You know how high I hold his

poetical reputation, but besides, one is naturally forced upon so many points of delicate consideration, that really I have begun and left off several times, and after all send the article to you with full power to cancel it if you think any part of it has the least chance of hurting his feelings. You know him better than I do, and you also know the public, and are aware that to make any successful impression on them the critic must appear to speak with perfect freedom. I trust I have not abused this discretion. I am sure I have not meant to do so, and yet during Lord Byron's absence, and under the present circumstances, I should feel more grieved than at anything that ever befell me if there should have slipped from my pen anything capable of giving him pain.

There are some things in the critique which are necessarily and unavoidably personal, and sure I am if he attends to it, which is unlikely, he will find advantage from

THE GREATEST OF ALL WORKS'

doing so. I wish Mr Gifford and you would consider every word carefully. If you think the general tenor is likely to make any impression on him, if you think it likely to hurt him either in his feelings or with the public, in God's name fling the sheets in the fire and let them be as <u>not written</u>. But if it appears, I should wish him to get an early copy, and that you would at the same time say I am the author, at your opportunity. No one can honour Lord Byron a genius more than I do, and no one had so great a wish to love him personally, though personally we had not the means of becoming very intimate. In his family distress (deeply to be deprecated, and in which probably he can yet be excused) I still looked to some moment of reflection when bad advisers (and, except you were one, I have heard of few whom I should call good) were distant from the side of one who is so much the child of feeling and emotion. An opportunity was once afforded me of interfering, but things appeared to me to have gone too far; yet, even after all, I wish I had tried it, for Lord Byron always seemed to give me credit for wishing him sincerely well, and knew me to be superior to what Commodore Trunnion would call the pigs-kitchen brash of literary envy and petty rivalry.

I got your letter in the country but was able to do nothing till I came to town both because I was occupied all day in my agricultural improvements & on account of certain curious cramps in the stomach which occupied three nights very ungraciously & threatened to send me out of this excellent world upon very short warning.

I have pressed Erskine to undertake the novel with all the arguments I can use & trust I shall succeed as I have offered him all the accumulated lore which I am possessed of to facilitate his labour. I find James Ballantyne had already spoke

to him on the subject. I only returned from Abbotsford last
Saturday very unwell but am now as stout as when – [The
rest of the sentence and the signature are cut away.]

Lawyer William Erskine, Lord Kinneder, was Scott's friend and
assisted him in his anonymous review of his own anonymously
published novel *Tales of My Landlord*.

The *Quarterly Review* continued to thrive commercially and
critically, although not all were entirely pleased with its quality
or focus, which at times could be compromised by the need
to meet the due publication date.

'Philomath' to the editor of the Quarterly Review, *17 August 1822*

Sir

I have been accustom'd for many years to read your
Quarterly Review. I mean to peruse one more, & to continue,
or discontinue the work, if I find you inclined to pay attention to, or disregard the remarks I am about to make.

So far from thinking you unequal to the task of a reviewer,
I conceive you to possess talents & acquirements every way
requisite for conveying valuable information. What I object to,
is that the publications you select for animadversion are so
utterly destitute of interest, that the time & expence laid out
in the perusal are utterly thrown away.

In these, I know, I am expressing the sentiments of many
of your subscribers in this neighbourhood, who, you will
find, will follow my example, unless they see an immediate
alteration. Is the life of Pitt, Sheridan, Blunt's tour, & other
works of equal merit to be overlooked, & nothing submitted

to public notice but what is utterly worthless? Such forms
the contents of your last Review, which instead of 6 shillings
is deemed not to be worth six pence.

I am, Sir

Yours

Philomath

The American writer Washington Irving penned histories,
biographies, satires, humorous works and short stories, the
most famous of which are probably 'Rip Van Winkle' (1819)
and 'The Legend of Sleepy Hollow' (1820). In 1817 he arrived
at Murray's with letters of introduction from Thomas Campbell
and Walter Scott, and thereafter Murray's published many of
Irving's works including the above stories in his *The Sketch
Book of Geoffrey Crayon, Gent* (1819–20).

Irving was very much interested in Spain and travelled there
extensively, eventually being appointed America's ambassador to
Spain. His access to extensive archives and histories informed a
prolific output, including the multi-volume *A History of the Life
and Voyages of Christopher Columbus* (1828), *Chronicle of the Conquest
of Granada* (1829) and *Tales of the Alhambra* (1832). Irving was
therefore well placed to review in the *Quarterly Review* fellow
American Alexander Slidell Mackenzie's *A Year in Spain* (1831).

*Washington Irving to John Murray III, Argyll Street, London,
6 April 1831*

My Dear John

As I am sending off dispatches &c to the United States
today, I should be glad to have the reviews of the 'Year in
Spain' about which you spoke.

Though communicating mere empty praises to an author is something like 'filling a man's belly with the East Wind', yet it may do for the present, until your father shall make up his mind as to the 'handsome thing' to be done in the matter, according to your intimation to me prior to my preparing the work for the press.

Yours very truly
Washington Irving

Elizabeth Rigby, afterwards Lady Eastlake, was a close friend of the Murrays – indeed it was at No. 50 that she became engaged. Murray's published her travel works such as *A Residence on the Shores of the Baltic* (1841) which were much admired, but her forte was as a reviewer, essayist and art critic. In *Handbook to Painting* she was insightful in discussing a wide range of European artists. She was also a notable early advocate of photography and argued for it to be considered a new artistic form. Her husband, Sir Charles Lock Eastlake, was also influential as president of the Royal Academy and director of the National Gallery. She was one of the few female contributors to the *Quarterly Review*, whose editor John Gibson Lockhart greatly admired her, writing to Murray III: 'I have no doubt she is the cleverest female writer now in England, the most original in thought and expression too, and she seems good besides, which after all has its charms for old sinners like you and me.' Her notable reviews included a savaging of Charlotte Brontë's *Jane Eyre* (1847) and a furious attack on John Ruskin's *Modern Painters* (1843–60). On the death of John Murray II she sent her commiserations to his son.

Elizabeth Rigby, afterwards Lady Eastlake, to John Murray III, Edinburgh, 5 September 1843

My Dear Mr Murray

It is with very mournful feelings that I find myself addressing another Mr Murray, though at the same time I feel that I can pay no more grateful homage to your dear father's memory than by expressing my entire regard & respect for his son. May that son ever reap the benefit of his own & his father's good sense. I must beg you to accept my thanks for your kind expressions, & I trust long to enjoy that friendship with your family which I consider the best fruits of my connection with Mr Murray as a publisher. That you all consider Mrs Murray decidedly better is indeed welcome news. I truly hope that Albemarle Street is destined long to be the scene of the best kind of happiness to herself & her family.

Your wishes & those of Mr Lockhart that I should continue to be a contributor to the Quarterly are in every way gratifying and flattering to me. But I hope by this time that you quite understand that in many matters which writers for the Quarterly are supposed to have at their finger's ends I am perfectly ignorant & shall probably always remain so. In addition also to a very deficient education, I do not lead, nor wish to lead, that life which should keep me au courant du jour. But such thoughts as a woman of the most private station & habits may have, & those plainly spoken, will ever be at your service, & you & Mr Lockhart are only too good to be pleased with them. I will do my best to mend the sheets you have sent me, but this catalogue is a very troublesome matter & one in which I want help which now I cannot command. Thank you for the coming books – I will endeavour to ascertain whether there are more which it might benefit me to see. Could you also obtain for me the address of Mrs [Sarah] Austin – or is there any person of your own acquaintance who could give me a little information respecting those extraordinary Berlin ladies – Rachel, Bettina & Charlotte Stieglitz – further than what appears in their most extraordinary biographies & letters? I know that their private histories are matters of public conversation in . . .

[second page missing]

Murray consulted John Gibson Lockhart on Alexander William Kinglake, who wrote *Eothen* (1844), described by the author as 'a description of adventures past, & impressions received during a tour of some duration in Turkey, Asia Minor, Syria, Palestine, & Egypt. The work is strictly true in its narrations, but it is marked so strongly by the impress of the writer's mind, & is so strongly imbued with his personal tastes, & feelings that it would hardly be fair perhaps to offer it to the public as a solid "book of travels".' Murray and Lockhart agreed that the work's irreverent style was inappropriate but that Kinglake might still be useful as a reviewer. Murray was one of twenty publishers to reject the title, which he later described as the 'worst blunder of his publishing life', as it went on to have over sixty printings. Murray published one of these editions.

Alexander William Kinglake to John Murray III, Taunton, 30 September 1844

Dear Sir

I beg to thank you very sincerely for your letter, & for the kind suggestions which it contains.

I am much pleased & flattered to hear that the editor of

the Quarterly has formed a favourable opinion of my book, & the more so since I feel that the absence of a strong purpose is a fault which may fairly have exposed it to severe remarks; the truth is that the course of events in the East deprived me of any graver motives for writing on the affairs of the Levant, & at last I was induced, as it were, to show the mere 'dress & scenery' without the drama.

It will give me much pleasure to comply with your request, by furnishing or attempting to furnish an occasional contribution to the Quarterly Review & I should be glad to hear from you whether there are any particular subjects on which you think it probable that my pen might be successfully employed. It occurs to me that a sketch of Louis Philippe's eventful life, written in a picturesque, & lively, but not malicious style might possibly be acceptable to the public. I am not a great reader of periodical literature, & am not sure therefore whether this ground has been occupied. I have no right to assume that I am capable of writing an article on this subject worthy of the Quarterly, but if you wish it, I will willingly make the experiment. I don't know that there is extant any good 'life' of the Citizen King. Wright's book, tho' containing many interesting facts, is a poor production.

I am, Dear Sir
Very truly yours
Alex W. Kinglake

Kinglake's first articles for the *Quarterly Review* were in fact on the 'Rights of Women' (December 1844) and 'The Mediterranean a French lake' (March 1845). Murray later published the first two volumes of his eight-volume *The Invasion of the Crimea* (1862), but they fell out over publishing differences and the remaining six volumes were published by William Blackwood (1863–87). Murray, again, rued his decision as the work was a huge success, making a profit of more than £20,000 by the end of the century.

One rule of the *Quarterly Review* was to prohibit the reproduction of its articles elsewhere. This led to a confrontation with railway writer Sir Francis Bond Head who wished to republish his own articles in a separate book. He wrote to John Murray III in 1848, saying: 'I do not know what are the rules of the Quarterly, but your father's rule was to make it a rule to do whatever I asked him to do. He would have boiled his boots and fried his trousers if I had recommended it. Until he struck his flag we were always quarrelling about trifles, but after a desperate battle he determined to sail on the other tack, and to the last hour of his valued life we were the best of friends. I never injured his boots or trousers; on the contrary, the more he trusted me, the more careful I was of him. Now, my dear sir, you must undergo the same ordeal, and rest quite satisfied that, in spite of all you say, you will republish my article . . . The first time I come to London I will call in Albemarle Street and settle it with you in a yard-arm conversation.' Murray backed down and even republished the railway articles himself as *Stokers and Pokers* (1849).

As the nineteenth century progressed, the widespread availability of political news and opinions in print through the medium of newspapers, journals and magazines made periodicals that appeared only four times a year seem increasingly old-fashioned. The *Quarterly Review* editor Whitwell Elwin was aware of the competition from other, more regular, publications and suggested a remedy to Murray.

Reverend Whitwell Elwin to John Murray III, Booton, Norwich, 18 October 1854

My Dear Murray

I read Johnstone's book some time ago with reference to the question of his capability to furnish us with an occasional political article. His essay appeared to me to want brilliancy and power, & unless in a case of extremity I doubt the policy of appealing to him. We must not forget that the Quarterly Reviewers are not in the same position with regard to politics as when they were first started. The daily papers have made immense advances since in their mode of treating subjects. They almost exhaust the topic before we approach it, and if to the advantage of novelty they are to add that of superior, potent argument & style our lucubrations will fall very flat in the public ear. Such latterly has actually been the case. For the last few years the political essays in the Quarterly & Edinburgh Review have been spoken of with little respect. If we are to restore interest to this part of our journal it must be by the employment of first ability. In ~~addition to~~ conjunction with this (for nothing will avail without it) we should with many disadvantages have some advantages also: we can treat subjects in their integrity in one consecutive paper, & by the longer intervals between our issues we can keep clear of many errors & passions to which those are exposed who write from day to day. I trust a good deal to our lofty, impartial tone for winning respect to our political opinions. There is no domestic question at present before the public, none which would attract the faintest interest, & our Christmas fare must be the [Crimean] war.

I doubt too the policy of an article at present on the Cathedral Commission. I talked the question over with [Dean] Stanley who cannot see his way. Neither can I and I should be sorry to commit ourselves prematurely. Add to this Robertson is a heavy writer, & the topic in his hands would be lead itself. At any rate we have so many papers on general subjects bespoke for Christmas as the number will carry. What we want now are lighter articles. Do not forget to send Clerical Economics to your brother-in-law.

I have sent [William] Harness's letter to Forrester who is a friend of his. Also a note which I got this morning from [Henry] Brougham who is at Paris, & who is vastly delighted with Foote. I have told Forrester to send you both, your own Harness, my Brougham. The last return to me when you have received & read it.

I have sent out all the cheques except Brougham's which I must keep till I receive his directions how to dispose of it.

I am going to Melton for the day & can say no more except that Lord Aberdeen ought not to be suffered to walk abroad without a muzzle.

Ever
Most sincerely yours
W. Elwin

Owing to the prestige and influence it was seen to have, and the lucrative remuneration it offered, many members of the public still wished to write for the *Quarterly Review*. One such was a certain Thomas Timoney, writing in a satirical vein.

Thomas J. Timoney to the editor of the Quarterly Review, *Ayot House, Herts, 12 March 1947*

Sir

Being at present disengaged (the fact is I have never as yet been engaged) I have no objection to tender my services for the advantage of your respectable journal. I do not much care what you require me to do, being equally able to perform all tasks great or small. Indeed, if agreeable to you I should rather like to do a bit of everything. I write essays offhand on all subjects. I am particularly liable to be struck by the minutest errors in any literary work, and am particularly slow at comprehending the author's meaning or the beauty of his work.

If the work is a scientific one I can charge the author with not treating his subject in a literary manner, and if the work is a literary one I can charge him with not treating it scientifically. From this you can estimate my capacity for your book reviews.

I am aware of the fact that your esteemed journal publishes neither fiction nor poetry, but nevertheless I deem it necessary to tell you that I can make poetry standing on one leg. I can find fault with both the modern poets and those that are traditional in manner.

I can criticise all plays ancient or modern. I can praise Pinero and deride Ben Jonson. I can exalt T. S. Eliot to the clouds and laugh at Shakespeare. Thus you can perceive how well I would do as a dramatic critic.

I have no doubt that after this you will put me on the staff of your review. If you do not I will become a literary genius just to spite you and, when I am wealthy I will buy the 'Quarterly Review' just for the pleasure of giving you a lecture on the crime of ignoring young literary aspirants.

I have one fault I must confess to you: I cannot spell; of course if mistakes in spelling ever occur in my articles, and they are bound to, you can blame them on the unfortunate printer.

One thing more. I was nineteen years of age on the 26th of February, my favourite author is Sir Walter Scott, and my favourite colour is grey.

I enclose a stamped and addressed envelope for your immediate reply, which I anxiously await. Until I receive it you can boast that,

I am your most

Humble servant to command

Thomas J. Timoney

John Murray V replied the next day, that 'according to your own account you seem to have many useful qualities, but I regret there is no vacancy on my staff, nor is there any prospect of one, and every week I receive similar applications.'

4

'C. has forged a letter in my name'
Caroline Lamb

———•———

Lady Caroline Lamb, an Anglo-Irish aristocrat, was the wife of William Lamb, later Viscount Melbourne and Queen Victoria's first prime minister. She found some fame as a novelist, though her literary career was overshadowed by her brief but tempestuous affair with Lord Byron in 1812. Afterwards she found it impossible to get over the relationship and remained obsessed by the man she infamously described as 'mad, bad and dangerous to know'. Byron placed in Murray's safekeeping a portrait miniature of himself that he intended as a gift to his mistress, Lady Oxford. Shortly after their break-up, Caro forged a letter, as if from Byron, in an attempt to obtain it for herself.

Lady Caroline Lamb, née Ponsonby, pretending to be Lord Byron, to John Murray II, January 1813

Once more, my dearest friend, let me assure you I had no hand in the satire you mention so do not take affront about nothing but call where I desired – as to refusing you the picture – it is quite ridiculous – only name me or if you like it then but this note & that will suffice – you know my reasons for wishing them not to allow all who call the same latitude; explain whatever you think necessary to them and

take which picture you think most like but do not forget to
return it the soonest you can – for reasons I explained. My
dearest friend take care of [deleted line] Byron

This letter was subsequently annotated by Byron: 'This letter
was forged in my name by Caroline L. for the purpose of
obtaining a picture from the hands of Mr M. – January 1813
Byron.' It is surprising that Murray, who received more letters
from Byron than anyone else, was duped by this forgery, especially as Caro's attempt to imitate Byron's flowing poetic style
of prose writing resulted in a disjointed and clumsy text.

Byron wrote to Lady Melbourne, his close friend and Caro's
mother-in-law, on 9 January 1813: 'C. by her own confession
has <u>forged</u> a <u>letter</u> in my <u>name</u> (the hand she imitates to perfection) & thus obtained from Mr Murray in Albemarle Street the
picture.' He also wrote to Murray.

*Lord Byron to John Murray II, Eywood, Presteign, Herefordshire,
8 January 1813*

Dear Sir

You have been imposed upon by a letter forged in my
name to obtain the picture left in your possession. This I
know by the confession of the culprit, & as she is a woman
(& of rank) with whom I have unfortunately been too much
connected you will for the present say little about it, but if

you have the letter <u>retain</u> it – & write to me the particulars. You will also be more cautious in future & not allow anything of mine to pass from your hands without my <u>seal</u> as well as signature. I have not been in town – nor have written to you since I left it – so I presume the forgery was a skilful performance. I shall endeavour to get back the picture by fair means if possible.

Ever yours
Byron

P.S. Keep the letter if you have it. I did not receive your parcel, it is now too late to send it as I shall be in town on the 17th. The <u>delinquent</u> is of one of the first families in this kingdom – but as Dogberry says this 'is flat burglary' – Favour me with an answer – I hear I am scolded in the Quarterly – but you & it are already forgiven – I suppose that made you bashful about sending it.

Byron also wrote to his close friend John Cam Hobhouse, diarist and radical politician, on 17 January 1813, that Caro 'has been <u>forging letters</u> in my name & hath thereby pilfered the best picture of <u>me</u>, the Newstead miniature!!! Murray was imposed upon. The Devil, & Medea, & her Dragons to boot, are possessed of that little maniac.'

⇾⇾⇾⇽⇽⇽

Caro's relationship with John Murray II lasted much longer than that with Byron and she was a frequent caller at 50 Albemarle Street. Murray too was obsessed with Byron and had a wax seal made with his portrait. The following letter is typical of Caro – a ramble, with little regard to coherence or punctuation.

'C. HAS FORGED A LETTER IN MY NAME'

Lady Caroline Lamb to John Murray II, 12 December 1816

It is strange but my visit to your house today has made me miserable – after all what a life mine has been & how irregular our acquaintance. You must show me the seal when it is done & the sketch of it before – I believe none will be found better to take the likeness from than Westall's print – The Journal you mentioned – were you serious, if indeed you will permit me to look at it I will call on you & read it – I had a thousand things to say to you but they were all forgotten the moment they said you were at home – is not life strange – whatever he is, however I have abused him – If I believed him at any hour unhappy would I not go through the fire to serve him & that child of his – will it be like him – but what is all this to me – your room speaks of him in every part of it – and I never see you without pain – yet is it not strange it seems to me most unpleasant if I pass any length of time without seeing you & what I can safely say – I add – That I think you have been a sincere upright & manly friend to both him & me – through many very trying scenes – if ever you are grieved send for me – for I am yours in my heart & soul – & perhaps I reproach myself for the violence with which I have presumed to judge & condemn another – of all people on earth I am the last to do so – whoever knew so little as myself how to command my own actions yet be approved. Whatever my faults I feel your kindness with the utmost gratitude & never never shall forget to name you amongst my real friends – if you should either in the morning or evening have a few moments to spare perhaps you will come here & when you do like to share me the journal – remember – that you can confer on me the greatest favour you can – yours C. L.

A few years later, on hearing the rumour that Byron had returned to Britain, Caro wrote once more to Murray a letter almost incoherent with excitement.

Lady Caroline Lamb, to John Murray II, Brockett Hall,
August 1820

My Dear Sir

You have never written to tell me about him now did you know the pain & agony this has given me you had not been so remiss [tell] me how he looks, what he says, if he be grown fat if he is no uglier than he used to be if in good-humoured or cross-grained putting his brows down – if his hair curls or is straight as somebody said, if he has seen Hobhouse, if he is going to stay long, if you went to Dover as you intended and a great deal more which if you had the smallest <u>tact</u> or aught else you would have written long ago, for as to me I shall certainly not see him neither do I care he should know that I ever asked him only – it is from mere curiosity I should like to hear all you can tell me about him – pray come here immediately.

Yours
C. L.

5

'The Ettrick Bard'
James Hogg

———◆———

The largely self-taught Scottish poet James Hogg, known as 'the Ettrick Shepherd', struggled to make a living as a shepherd and enjoyed only limited commercial success as a writer, with such poems as *The Queen's Wake* (1813). Despite gaining admirers among literary circles, his lack of manners and argumentative nature often caused him difficulties. As a result he was always short of money and hoped that his friendships with John Murray II, Walter Scott and Lord Byron would boost his literary career. Byron wrote to Murray to support his fellow poet.

Lord Byron to John Murray II, Hastings, 3 August 1814

Dear Sir

It is certainly a little extraordinary that you have not sent the E[dinburgh] R[eview], as I requested, and hoped it would not require a note a day to remind you. I see <u>advertisements</u> of Lara and Jaqueline; pray, <u>why</u>? when I requested you to postpone publication till my return to town. [two lines crossed out]

I have a most amusing epistle from the Ettrick Bard Hogg – in which, speaking of his bookseller, whom he denominates the 'shabbiest' of the <u>trade</u> for not 'lifting his bills', he adds, in so many words, 'G-d d-n him and them both.' This is a pretty prelude to asking you to adopt him (the said Hogg) but this he wishes – and if you please, you and I will talk it over. He has a poem ready for the press (and your <u>bills</u> too, if '<u>liftable</u>'), and bestows some benedictions on Mr Moore for his abduction of Lara from the forthcoming Mis[cellany].

Yours ever

B.

P.S. Seriously, I think Mr Hogg would suit you very well; and surely he is a man of great powers, and deserving of encouragement. I must knock out a tale for him, and you should at all events consider before you reject his suit. Scott is gone to the Orkneys in a gale of wind; and Hogg says that, during the said gale, 'he is sure that S. is not quite at his ease, to say the best of it.' Ah! I wish these home-keeping bards could taste a Mediterranean white squall, or the Gut in a gale of wind, or even the Bay of Biscay with no wind at all.

Hogg, however, often caused offence to his fellow poets: with Byron by making crude and inappropriate jokes over his marriage and with Scott and Byron over their reluctance to contribute to his proposed poetical magazine.

Hogg and Murray first met in Edinburgh in the autumn of 1814, with Murray encouraged to publish him upon his reciting part of his poem *Pilgrims of the Sun* (1815). Between the agreement to publish and the work appearing in print Hogg, desperate for money and news of Byron, wrote to Murray.

James Hogg to John Murray II, Edinburgh, 26 December 1814

Dear Murray

What the deuce have you made of my excellent poem that you are never publishing it while I am starving for want of money and cannot even afford a Christmas goose to my friends? I think I may say of you as the countryman said to his friend who asked him when his wife had her accouchement 'Troth, man' said he 'she's aye gaun aboot yet and I think she'll be gaun to keep this ane till hirsel a thegither'. However I daresay that like the said wife you have your reasons for it but of all things a bookseller's reasons suit worst with a poets board – I should be glad to know if you got safely across the Tweed and what number of the little family group you lost by the way betwixt Edin. and London and how everything in the literary world is going on with you since that time – Why do you never write to me? Have you ever seen Moore or talked to him about our projected reporting? What in the world is become of that unlucky perverse callan Lord Byron? I have not heard from him these two months and more. I have really been afraid for some time past that he was dead or perhaps even married and was truly very concerned about the lad – But I was informed the other day by a gentleman of the utmost respectability that he was very busy writing godly psalms to be sung in congregations and families and when I heard that I said, 'If that be the case there's no man sure of his life' – I do not know_where to find him else I would write him a scolding letter – I have nothing in the world to say to you only be sure to let me hear from you and tell me how you are like to come on with the copies of the Queen's Wake which I sent you. It has been a losing

business and you must get me as much for it as you can
afford. I hope you will soon find occasion for sending me
an offer for a fifth edition. I am interrupted so farewell for
the present.

God bless you
James Hogg

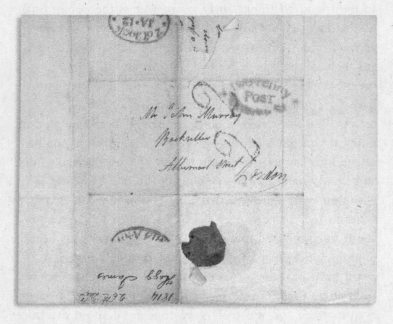

On 7 April 1815 Murray engineered the first meeting between
the two greatest literary figures of the day: Walter Scott and Lord
Byron. Murray wrote to Hogg on 10 April of the momentous
event: 'This I consider as a commemorative event in literary history
& I sincerely regret that you were not present – I wish to
God you had dash'd up to London at once and if you will
do so immediately I will undertake to board you if you will get
a bed.'

While Murray was able to supply Hogg with money from

his publications, Hogg's thoughts were turning to a more lucrative solution: a wealthy wife.

James Hogg to John Murray II, Edinburgh, 7 May 1815

My Dear Sir

I thank you with all my heart for the little timeous
supply you have lent me at present. I did intend shortly to
have asked from you what little you could spare from the
copies of <u>the Wake</u> sold, but I had no thought that the final
payment of the Pilgrims would have been made to me
sooner than November. You are the prince of booksellers if
people would but have you to your own judgement and
natural generous disposition. I offered Blackwood a regular
receipt for the full payment made by you of the first edition
of the Pilgrims but he declined it saying the bills were of
themselves a sufficient receipt – I leave Edin. on Thursday
for my little farm on Yarrow. I will have a confused summer
for I have as yet no house that I can dwell in but I hope by
and by to have some fine fun there with you fishing in Saint
Mary's Lake and Yarrow, eating bull trouts, singing songs and
drinking whisky. This little possession is what I stood much
in need of, a habitation among my native hills was what of
all the world I desired and if I had a little more money at
command I would just be as happy a man as I know of, but
that is an article of which I am ever in want. I wish you or
Mrs Murray would speer me out a good wife with a few
thousands; I daresay there is many a romantic girl about
London who would think it a fine play to become a Yarrow
shepherdess.

I suppose I must give up thoughts of further publication
for the summer. Contrive however to keep me before the

public – 'out o' sight out o' mind', I hear of nothing in the literary world very interesting except that people are commending some of Lord Byron's melodies as incomparably beautiful and laughing immoderately at Mr Wordsworth's new prefaces which certainly excel all that ever was written in this world in egotism, vanity and absurdity.

If Scott is still in London remember me to him and tell him I would fain see him before I leave town as I want particularly to consult him about some country affairs.

Believe me, dear Murray, very

And sincerely yours

James Hogg

Murray was unable, or unwilling, to find Hogg a wife. However, in 1820 Hogg wed Margaret Phillips, a daughter of a prosperous Dumfriesshire farmer, and they enjoyed a happy marriage with four daughters and a son. His financial situation did improve, although he still struggled and regularly chased his publishers for money.

6

Emma
Jane Austen

———◆———

J ane Austen enjoyed only modest success as a novelist with her early works, *Sense and Sensibility* (1811), *Pride and Prejudice* (1813) and *Mansfield Park* (1814), published by the military specialist Thomas Egerton. She therefore decided that a more literary and popular publisher would provide the greater success she craved. John Murray's standing made him her preferred publisher; later on she was to refer to him as 'a rogue of course, but a civil one'.

Fortunately, the normally acerbic literary adviser William Gifford admired Austen's books and encouraged Murray to publish her. In the following letter, which deals with many other publishing matters, Gifford was scathing about an anonymous novelist whose manuscript he thought contained many defects.

William Gifford to John Murray II, 21 November 1814

My Dear Sir

The translation is spirited and in a great measure correct – but the author shall look it over once more very carefully, as there are several French terms rather idiomatic and a few French expressions – but my opinion of the whole is favourable.

Of the novel, I hardly know what to say – it improves;
but there are radical defects. The writer has copied models of
which the world is tired: and she has <u>descriptions</u> of characters which she wants strength to fill up. Her chief man is a
failure. He is described as stern, commanding, dignified & yet
his language is mean & his conduct vulgar. There is little
knowledge of the world, and none of the language of high
life. With all this, it has much merit in particular places: and
some of the characters are prettily drawn. It begins with too
much bluster, & the old Lord who makes such a figure in
the outset dwindles into a very poor person in the scene, I
think not!

The style wants compression, & I have made a few
scratches in the opening pages to point out what seems
necessary to be done. Briefly, the lady (for I presume the
writer is a lady) wants a <u>severe friend</u>. With his assistance she
might rise far above the herd of novel writers, for she has
talents, and a facility of expression; but this is a <u>sine qua non</u>.
The novel will be read, but it will not last.

I have for the first time looked into 'Pride and Prejudice'
& it is really a very pretty thing. No dark passages – no
secret chambers, no wind howling in long galleries; no drops
of blood upon a rusty dagger – things that should now be
left to lady's maids and sentimental washerwomen.

I enclose a bit for Roworth from Dr G. – I am just as
anxious to get on as you can wish me – but I hear nothing
from Southey yet.

You have no conscience – to complain about America! I
am so pleased with Sir G. Prevost for not surrendering the
army, as I always imagined he would do, that I think his
merely running away places him ~~places him~~ in the very first
rank of patriots & heroes.

Remember that I can say nothing as to chance of popularity of Le [word unclear] It is certainly amusing, & now the times are calmer, people may like to look back upon other ages. This you can judge of better than I can.

My Dear Sir

Yours &c

W. G.

I have kept back the 4th vol. of the MS novel – meaning to read it, at least to look it through this evening – I assure you I have read very hard. Tomorrow you may have it.

As was typical of Austen's day men tended to look after business matters, and Jane's brother Henry assumed this role for her. Despite illness, he dictated this letter regarding Murray's opinion of Austen and his offer for her works, including the previously published *Sense and Sensibility* and *Mansfield Park* and her new work *Emma* (1816). Murray offered £450 for all her copyrights; she turned this down, preferring to take the risk of publishing on commission, with Murray receiving a modest 10 per cent of net sales.

Henry Austen to John Murray II, London, 21 October 1815

Dear Sir

Severe illness has confined me to my bed ever since I received yours of ye 15th – I cannot yet hold a pen, & employ an amanuensis. The politeness & perspicuity of your letter equally claim my earliest exertion. Your official opinion of the merits of Emma is very valuable & satisfactory. Though I venture occasionally from your critique, yet I assure you that the quantum of your commendation

rather exceeds than falls short of the author's expectation &
my own. The terms you offer are so very inferior to what
we had expected, that I am apprehensive of having made
some great error in my arithmetical calculation. On the
subject of the expense & profit of publishing, you must be
much better informed than I am; but documents in my
possession appear to prove that the sum offered by you for
the copyright of Sense & Sensibility, Mansfield Park &
Emma, is not equal to the money which my sister has
actually cleared by one very moderate edition of Mansfield
Park (you yourself expressed astonishment that so small an
edition of such a work should have been sent into the
world) & still a smaller one of Sense & Sensibility.
[remainder of letter missing]

Her brother's continuing illness meant that Jane Austen herself
took on direct dealings with Murray. In this letter she suggested
that since her novel, *Emma*, was dedicated to the Prince Regent
it shouldn't have to suffer from printing delays.

Jane Austen to John Murray II, Hans Place, London,
23 November 1815

Sir

My brother's note last Monday has been so fruitless, that
I am afraid there can be little chance of my writing to any
good effect; but yet I am so very much disappointed &
vexed by the delays of the printers that I cannot help
begging to know whether there is no hope of their being
quickened. Instead of the work being ready by the end of
the present month, it will hardly, at the rate we now

proceed, be finished by the end of the next, and as I expect to leave London early in December, it is of consequence that no more time should be lost. Is it likely that the printers will be influenced to greater dispatch & punctuality by knowing that the work is to be dedicated, by permission, to the Prince Regent? If you can make that circumstance operate, I shall be very glad. My brother returns [Walter Scott's] Waterloo, with many thanks for the loan of it. We have heard much of Scott's account of Paris; if it be not incompatible with other arrangements, would you favour us with it – supposing you have any set already opened? You may depend upon its being in careful hands.

I remain, Sir

Your obedient humble servant

J. Austen

Under Austen's publishing agreement with Murray, she was responsible for all publishing costs including those for a handsomely bound copy to be presented to the Prince Regent.

Jane Austen to John Murray II, London, 11 December 1815

Dear Sir

As I find that *Emma* is advertised for publication as early as Saturday next, I think it best to lose no time in settling all that remains to be settled on the subject, & adopt this method of doing so, as involving the smallest tax on your time.

In the first place, I beg you to understand that I leave the terms on which the trade should be supplied with the work, entirely to your judgment, entreating you to be guided in every such arrangement by your own experience of what is most likely to clear off the edition rapidly. I shall be satisfied with whatever you feel to be best.

The title page must be, Emma, Dedicated by Permission to H.R.H. The Prince Regent. And it is my particular wish that one set should be completed & sent to H.R.H. two or three days before the work is generally public – it should be sent under cover to the Rev. J. S. Clarke, Librarian, Carleton House. I shall subjoin a list of those persons, to whom I must trouble you to forward also a set each, when the work is out; all unbound, with <u>From the Authoress</u> in the first page.

I return you, with very many thanks, the books you have so obligingly supplied me with. I am very sensible to assure you of the attention you have paid to my convenience & amusement. I return also Mansfield Park, as ready for a second edition, I believe, as I can make it.

I am in Hans Place till the 16th. From that day, inclusive, my direction will be, Chawton, Alton, Hants.

I remain, Dear Sir

Your faithful humble servant

J. Austen

I wish you would have the goodness to send a line by the bearer, stating the <u>day</u> on which the set will be ready for the Prince Regent.

Although Murray was only publishing Austen's works on commission he did his utmost to promote the novels and encouraged Walter Scott to review them, writing in December 1815: 'Have you any fancy to dash off an article on Emma? It wants incident and romance & imagination – does it not – none of the author's other novels have been noticed & surely Pride & Prejudice merits high consideration.' Scott's positive and sympathetic review duly appeared and Austen wrote appreciatively of all Murray's efforts in publishing *Emma*, alluding also to the devastating bankruptcy of her brother Henry, with whom Murray had initially dealt.

Jane Austen to John Murray II, Chawton, 1 April 1816

Dear Sir

I return to you the Quarterly Review with many thanks. The authoress of Emma has no reason I think to complain of her treatment in it – except in the total omission of Mansfield Park. I cannot but be sorry that so clever a man as the reviewer of Emma, should consider it as unworthy of being noticed. You will be pleased to hear that I have received the Prince's thanks for the <u>handsome</u> copy I sent him of Emma. Whatever he may think of <u>my</u> share of the work, <u>yours</u> seems to have been quite right.

In consequence of the late sad event in Henrietta Street – I must request that if you should at any time have anything to communicate by letter, you will be so good as to write by the post, directing to me (Miss J. Austen), Chawton near Alton – and that for anything of a larger bulk, you will add to the same direction, <u>by Collier's Southampton Coach</u>.

I remain, Dear Sir

Yours very faithfully

J. Austen

Following Austen's early death in 1817, Murray published her posthumous *Northanger Abbey* and *Persuasion* (1818). All Jane's copyrights were inherited by her sister Cassandra and when these were approaching their expiry she entered into detailed negotiations about reissuing the novels, which to date had only had modest sales, but the discussions broke down. New editions of Austen's novels were eventually published by Richard Bentley.

7

'By the author of *Waverley*'
Walter Scott

———◆———

S ir Walter Scott, while a notable poet, ballad collector, anti-quarian, translator, correspondent, historian, biographer, essayist and reviewer, is principally regarded as a novelist. His internationally bestselling historical works, including *Waverley* (1814), *Rob Roy* (1817) and *Ivanhoe* (1819), established a new genre of historical fiction, which made his fortune. *Waverley* was published anonymously, partly in deference to the contemporary low standing of such fiction and its incompatibility with Scott's social position as the sheriff-depute (principal judge) of Selkirkshire and principal clerk to the Court of Session in Edinburgh.

Scott maintained his anonymity, with varying degrees of success, until a financial crisis in 1826 led to him publicly admitting the authorship. John Murray II, as publisher of some of Scott's non-fiction works, hoped to have the opportunity of publishing some of the lucrative Waverley Novels, which he suspected Scott had written. His chance came through his close association with William Blackwood, a publisher in Edinburgh who had recently consulted with James Ballantyne, printer of the Waverley Novels.

William Blackwood to John Murray II, Edinburgh, 12 April 1816

Most strictly confidential

My Dear Murray

Some time ago I wrote to you that James Ballantyne had dined with me, and from what then passed I expected that I would soon have something very important to communicate. He has now fully explained himself to me, with liberty to inform you of anything he has communicated. This, however, he entreats of us to keep most strictly to ourselves, trusting to our honour that we will not breathe a syllable of it to the dearest friends we have.

He began by telling me that he thought he had it now in his power to show me how sensible he was of the services I had done him, and how anxious he was to accomplish that union of interests which I had so long been endeavouring to bring about. Till now he had only made professions; now he would act. He said that he was empowered to offer me, along with you, a work of fiction in four volumes, such as Waverley, etc.; that he had read a considerable part of it; and, knowing the plan of the whole, he could answer for its being a production of the very first class; but that he was not at liberty to mention its title, nor was he at liberty to give the author's name. I naturally asked him, was it by the author of Waverley? He said it was to have no reference to any other work whatever, and everyone would be at liberty to form their own conjectures as to the author. He only requested that, whatever we might suppose from anything that might occur afterwards, we should keep strictly to ourselves that we were to be the publishers. The terms he was empowered by the author to offer for it were:

1. The author to receive one-half of the profits of each edition; these profits to be ascertained by deducting the paper and printing from the proceeds of the book sold at sale price; the publishers to be at the whole of the expense of advertising.

2. The property of the book to be the publishers', who were to print such editions as they chose.

3. The only condition upon which the author would agree to these terms is, that the publisher should take L600 of John Ballantyne's stock, selected from the list annexed, deducting 25 per cent from the affixed sale prices.

4. If these terms are agreed to, the stock to the above amount to be immediately delivered, and a bill granted at twelve months.

5. That in the course of six or eight weeks, J. B. expected to be able to put into my hands the first two volumes printed, and that if on perusal we did not like the bargain, we should be at liberty to give it up. This he considered to be most unlikely; but if it should be the case, he would bind himself to repay or redeliver the bill on the books being returned.

6. That the edition, consisting of 2,000 copies, should be printed and ready for delivery by the 1st of October next.

I have thus stated to you as nearly as I can the substance of what passed. I tried in various ways to learn something with regard to the author; but he was quite impenetrable. My own impression now is, that it must be Walter Scott, for

no one else would think of burdening us with such trash as
John B.'s wretched stock. This is such a burden, that I am
puzzled not a little. I endeavoured every way I could to get
him to propose other terms, but he told me they could not
be departed from in a single part; and the other works had
been taken on the same conditions, and he knew they would
be greedily accepted again in the same quarter.

Consider the matter seriously, and write to me as soon as
you can. After giving it my consideration, and making some
calculations, I confess I feel inclined to hazard the specula-
tion; but still I feel doubtful until I hear what you think of
it. Do not let my opinion, which may be erroneous, influence you, but judge for yourself. From the very strong terms
in which Jas. B. spoke of the work, I am sanguine enough to
expect it will equal if not surpass any of the others. I would
not lay so much stress upon what he says if I were not
assured that his great interest, as well as Mr Scott's, is to
stand in the very best way both with you and me. They are
anxious to get out of the clutches of Constable, and
Ballantyne is sensible of the favour I have done and may still
do him by giving so much employment, besides what he
may expect from you. From Constable he can expect
nothing. I had almost forgotten to mention that he assured
me in the most solemn manner that we had got the first
offer, and he ardently hoped we would accept of it. If,
however, we did not, he trusted to our honour that we
would say nothing of it; that the author of this work would
likely write more; and should we not take this, we might
have it in our power afterwards to do something with him,
provided we acted with delicacy in the transaction, as he had
no doubt we would do. I hope you will be able to write to
me soon, and as fully as you can. If I have time tomorrow,

or I should rather say this day, as it is now near one o'clock, I will write you about other matters; and if I have no letter from you, will perhaps give you another scolding.

Yours most truly

W. Blackwood

Blackwood and Murray agreed to Ballantyne's limited proposal on the copyright for *Tales of My Landlord* (1816) comprising *The Black Dwarf* and *The Tale of Old Mortality*, an edition of 6,000 copies only. The four volumes were published on 1 December 1816, without 'by the Author of *Waverley*' on the title page, but with few in doubt that it was indeed by the same hand, and the mystery of the author's identity still a matter of enquiry and discussion.

Murray wrote to Scott on 14 December 1816: 'Although I dare not address you as the author of certain Tales – which, however, must be written either by Walter Scott or the devil – yet nothing can restrain me from thinking that it is to your influence with the author of them that I am indebted for the essential honour of being one of their publishers; and I must intrude upon you to offer my most hearty thanks, not divided but doubled, alike for my worldly gain therein, and for the great acquisition of professional reputation which their publication has already procured me. As to delight, I believe I could, under any oath that could be proposed, swear that I never experienced such great and unmixed pleasure in all my life as the reading of this exquisite work has afforded me; and if you witnessed the wet eyes and grinning cheeks with which, as the author's chamberlain, I receive the unanimous and vehement praise of them from everyone who has read them, or heard the curses of those whose needs my scanty supply would not satisfy, you might judge of the sincerity with which I now entreat you to assure the author of the most complete success. After this, I could throw all the other books which I have in the press into the Thames, for no one will either read them or buy.'

Scott's reply attempted to disassociate himself from the authorship.

Walter Scott to John Murray II, Edinburgh, 18 December 1816

My Dear Sir

I give you heartily joy of the success of the Tales, although I do not claim that paternal interest in them, which my friends do me the credit to assign to me. I do assure I never read a volume of them till they were printed, & can only join with the rest of the world in applauding the true & striking portraits which they present of old Scottish manners. I do not expect implicit reliance to be placed on my disavowal, because I know very well that he who is resolved not to own a work, must necessarily deny it, & that otherwise his secret would be at the mercy of all who chose to ask the question since silence in such a case must always pass for consent, or rather assent. But I have a mode of convincing you that I am perfectly serious in my denial, pretty similar to that by which Solomon distinguished the fictitious from the real mother, & that is, by reviewing the work, which I take to be an operation similar to the experiment of quartering the child. But this is only on condition I can have W. Erskine's assistance, who admires the work greatly more than I do, though I think the painting of the second Tale both true & powerful. I knew old Mortality very well; his name was Paterson, but few knew him otherwise than by his nickname. The first Tale is not very original in its concoction, & lame & impotent in the conclusions.

My love to Gifford. I have been over head & ears in work this summer or I would have sent the Gypsies, indeed I was partly stop'd by finding it impossible to procure a few words of their language.

Constable wrote me about 2 months since desirous of having a new edition of Paul, but not hearing from you, I conclude you are still on hand, Longman's people had then only 60 copies.

Kind compliments to Heber whom I expected at Abbotsford this season, also to Mr Croker, & all your 4 o'clock visitors. I am just going to Abbotsford to make a small addition to my premises there. I have now about 700 acres thanks to the booksellers & the discerning public.

Yours truly

W. Scott

Edin 18 Dec

I have much to ask about Lord Byron, if I had time. His third canto is inimitable. Of the last poems there are one or two which indicate rather an irregular play of imagination. What a pity that a man of such exquisite genius will not be contented to be happy on the ordinary terms. I declare my heart bleeds when I think of him, self-banished from the country to which he is an honour.

Scott worried about Byron's reputation and sanity, having felt he had been unfairly treated by the British public, whose obsession with Byron, and scorn, had encouraged him to leave the country.

Scott enclosed in the letter his harsh review of his own *Tales*. By reviewing *Waverley* and the other Waverley Novels alongside the *Tales* the supposedly independent work became associated. His review of the two *Tales*, *The Black Dwarf* and *The Tale of Old Mortality*, endeavoured to put his publishers and readers off the scent by finding fault. Of *The Black Dwarf*, for example, he wrote: 'the narrative is unusually artificial; neither hero nor heroine excites interest of any sort, being just that sort of <u>pattern</u> people whom nobody cares a farthing about.' *Old Mortality* was also criticised as 'the author has cruelly falsified history', and we 'may charitably suggest that he was writing a romance, and not a history'. He ended his review with: 'We intended here to conclude this long article, when a strong report reached us of certain trans-Atlantic confessions, which, if genuine (though of this we know nothing), assign a different author to these volumes than the party suspected by our Scottish correspondents.' This was to support the suggestion that the author of the *Tales* was Scott's own brother. The deception worked on Murray who wrote to Blackwood on 15 February 1817: 'I will believe, till within an inch of my life, that the author of Tales of my Landlord is Thomas Scott.'

Once the agreed 6,000 copies of *Tales* had sold, the work reverted to Constable and was afterwards published with the other Waverley Novels.

More than a decade later, John Murray III was completing his education at the University of Edinburgh and was working as an apprentice with the publishers Oliver & Boyd; he was urged by his father to socialise too, as it was considered an essential part of a successful publishing career. His letters home were full of information and gossip from his studies, work experience and lively socialising. In 1827, Murray found himself attending a Theatrical Fund dinner, held at the Assembly Rooms on George Street, where Scott was forced publicly to declare himself the author. This revelation had been prompted by Scott's exposure to the financial collapse of his partners, the publisher Archibald Constable and the printers John and James Ballantyne. Among the attendees was Charles Mackay, an actor who became famous for his portrayal of Bailie Nicol Jarvie, a character from Scott's novel *Rob Roy*, which had been adapted for the stage.

John Murray III to John Murray II, Edinburgh,
26 February 1827

My Dear Sir

Your letter has made me perfectly happy, I am very much obliged to you for it, and am sure that when you find time you will again oblige me by letting me hear from you. I assure you that the receipt of a letter from you or from my mother is the greatest possible incentive to induce me to write. Captain Hall sets off tomorrow and will probably be the bearer of this. I was rather perplexed on receiving the enclosed without any instruction as to what was to be done with it; I have however conjectured for whom it was meant, and sent it to Captain Hall before I heard from you. I do not understand about the printing of it by Mr Ballantyne, owing to Captain Hall's sudden departure I fear he will not be able to read it over. I think he had better take it with him to town. Even before receiving your letter I had come to a determination of giving up a frequency of parties, both in compliance with the suggestion of Captain Hall and Dr Thomson, and also from finding that I could scarcely stand it, on the score of health; my 'dies fasti' then are to be Friday and Saturday. I take it very kind in you that you have been so very ready in complying with my request, of leaving to ride, and of having a paper sent to me; the latter will not only oblige me but Dr Thomson's family, and Miss Gilliland to whom I intended always to send it. I believe I mentioned to you that Mr Allan had kindly offered to take me with him to a Theatrical Fund dinner, which took place on Friday last. There were present about 300 persons – a mixed company, many of them not of the most respectable order. Sir Walter Scott took the chair, and there was scarcely another person of any note to support him except the actors. The dinner, therefore, would have been little better than endurable, had it not been remarkable for the confession of Sir Walter Scott that he was the author of the Waverley Novels.

This acknowledgment was forced from him, I believe, contrary to his own wish, in this manner. Lord Meadowbank, who sat on his left hand, proposed his health, and after paying him many compliments, ended his speech by saying that the clouds & mists which had so long surrounded the Great Unknown were now revealed, and he appeared in his true character (probably alluding to the exposé made before Constable's creditors, for I do not think there was any preconcerted plan). Upon this Sir Walter rose, and said, I did not expect on coming here today that I should have to disclose before 300 people a secret which, considering it had already been made known to about thirty persons, had been tolerably well kept. I am not prepared to give my reasons for preserving it a secret, caprice had certainly a great share in the matter. Now that it is out, I beg leave to observe that I am sole and undivided author of those novels. Every part of them has originated with me, or has been suggested to me in the course of my reading. I confess I am guilty, and am almost afraid to examine the extent of my delinquency. 'Look on't again, I dare not!'

The wand of Prospero is now broken, and my book is

buried, but before I retire I shall propose the health of a person who has given so much delight to all now present, the Bailie Nicol Jarvie. (I report this from memory.) Of course it is not quite accurate in words, but you will find a ~~further~~ tolerable report of it in the Caledonian Mercury of Saturday. This declaration was received with loud and long applause. As this was gradually subsiding the Bailie (Mackay) exclaiming in character Ma conscience if my father the Bailie had been alive &c, which, as you may suppose, had a most excellent effect. Mr Allan spoke but his oratory is not of the highest order. He at first would not take my money for the ticket, but as I would not consent to allow him to pay I sent it next day. I also subscribed a pound to the Fund so that my dinner was rather an expensive affair. Today I paid a visit to Mr [George] Boyd who returned Tuesday night; we had a long conversation respecting a subject which I dare say you have already discussed with him, viz my initiation into the bookselling business, when the chores are over, and I have more because I am to attend frequently at Oliver & Boyd's; the latter is to give me a desk in his own private room, and is gradually to instruct me in whatever will be useful for me to learn. I am particularly pleased with Mr Boyd from the kindnesses in which he received me & explained all their plans to me. He seems most particularly good natured. You ask me about my studies. I flatter myself I am getting on tolerably well with them, indeed I think I shall with your leave set up a laboratory, & mineralogical collection when I return home, and become a chemist & geologist. I fancy that I now begin to entertain less horror for arithmetic, and I intend to work with redoubled ardour at French & German. In fact I hope to have made some acquisition in knowledge of various kinds before you see me again. In chemistry & natural history I find [word missing] a new field open to me. I have several times attended the Wernerian Society through the kindness of Prof Jameson. I shall send him the <u>Sandwich Islands</u> tomorrow; would it be possible to get for him a copy of Brooke's new book, he was much pleased with his former work & has asked frequently for this. I have lately met several times a Mr Audubon, an American traveller and ornithologist who is here publishing a very splendid work on birds; he is shortly going to London, and will get letters to you if not from me, from Captain Hall who will tell you all about him; his conversation is particularly interesting. I was introduced to Mr Lizars who is engraving Mr Audubon's work, and am to go to his house to meet Mr Audubon on Wednesday evening (not to a party however). Captain Hall was kind enough to ask me to dine with him on Saturday, being engaged I could not accept the invitation. I hope you will assure him that I am most sensible of the great kindness, and attention I have received from him since my arrival in Edinburgh. I must now endeavour to write a few lines to my mother, to thank her for her great kindness in writing to me so often.

Believe me, my dear Father

Your dutiful & affectionate son

J. Murray

8

Don Juan
Lord Byron

———◆———

Though he had already published some juvenile and satirical poetry, it was *Childe Harold's Pilgrimage* (1812) that established Lord Byron's name and secured him immediate and enduring success. Based on his youthful travels in the Mediterranean, it introduced the largely autobiographical 'Byronic hero': misanthropic characters, weary of the world and anti-establishment. Byron's poetry and life became increasingly scandalous, culminating in his epic masterpiece *Don Juan*. Murray published the first two cantos anonymously in 1819 and Cantos III, IV and V in 1821. However, the further cantos were published elsewhere after Murray's impassioned plea to Byron to moderate their language and content failed. Byron's first draft of *Don Juan* included insulting satirical attacks on the Foreign Secretary Lord Castlereagh and the poet Robert Southey, which he agreed to omit. Byron wrote on the proof page of the dedication mocking Southey: 'As the Poem is to be published anonymously, omit the Dedication. I won't attack the dog in the dark. Such things are for scoundrels and renegadoes like himself.'

Lord Byron to John Murray II, Venice, 20 January 1819

Dear Sir

I write two lines to say that if you publish Don Juan – I

will only have the stanzas on Castlereagh <u>omitted</u> – and the two concluding words (Bob-Bob) of the two last lines of the third stanza of the dedication to S. I explained to Hobhouse why I have attacked that scoundrel & request him to explain to you the reason. The opinions which I have asked of Mr H. & others were with regard to the poetical merit – & not as to what they may think due to the cant of the day – which still reads the Bath Guide Little's poems – Prior – & Chaucer – to say nothing of Fielding & Smollett. If published – publish entire – with the above mentioned exceptions – or you may publish anonymously – or not at all – in the latter event print 50 on my account for private distribution.

Yours ever

B.

I have written by this post to Messrs K[innaird]. and H[obhouse]. to desire that they will not erase more than I have stated. The second canto of Don Juan is finished in 206 stanzas.

When submitting the second canto, Byron defiantly stated to Murray that he would accept no editorial interference. He also explained that his demand to remove the lines on Castlereagh was due to his not being in Britain and therefore unable to answer the inevitable challenge to a duel that would follow.

Lord Byron to John Murray II, Venice, 25 January 1819

Dear Sir

You will do me the favour to print privately – (for private distribution) fifty copies of Don Juan – the list of the men to whom I wish it to be presented I will send hereafter. The other two poems had best be added to the ~~rest~~ collective edition – I do not approve of <u>their</u> being published separately. <u>Print</u> Don Juan <u>entire</u> omitting of course the lines on Castlereagh as I am not on the spot to meet him. I have a second canto ready – which will be sent by & bye. By this post I have written to Mr Hobhouse – addressed to your care.

Yours ever truly
Byron

P.S. I have acquiesced in the request – & representation – & having done so – it is idle to ~~prot~~ detail my arguments in favour of my own self-love & 'Poeshie'; but I protest. If the poem has poetry – it would stand – if not – fall – the rest is 'leather & prunella', – and has never yet affected any human production 'pro or con'. Dullness is the only annihilator in such cases. As to the cant of the day – I despise it – as I have ever done all its other finical fashions, which become you as paint ~~upon~~ became the Antient Britons. If you admit this prudery – you must omit half Ariosto – La Fontaine – Shakespeare – Beaumont – Fletcher – Massinger – Ford – all the Charles second writers – in short <u>something</u> of ~~all~~ most who have written ~~since~~ before Pope – and are worth reading – and much of Pope himself – <u>read him</u> – most of you <u>don't</u> – but <u>do</u> – & I will forgive you – though the inevitable consequence would be that you would burn all I have ever written – and all your other wretched Claudians of the day (except Scott & Crabbe) into the bargain. I wrong Claudian who <u>was</u> a <u>poet</u> by naming him with such fellows – but he was the 'ultimus Romanorum' the tail of the comet – and these persons are the tail of an old gown cut into a waistcoat for Jackey – but being both <u>tails</u> – I have compared one with the other – though very unlike – like all similes. I write in a passion and a Sirocco – and was up till six this morning at the carnival; but I <u>protest</u> – as I did in my former letter.

As *Don Juan* approached publication, Byron became increasingly defensive of his work, resisting Murray's editing and over-management of the poem.

Lord Byron to John Murray II, Venice, 6 April 1819

Dear Sir

The second canto of Don Juan was sent on Saturday last by post in 4 packets – two of 4 – & two of three sheets each – containing in all two hundred & seventeen stanzas octave measure. But I will permit no curtailments except those mentioned about Castlereagh & the two '<u>Bobs</u>' in the introduction. You sha'n't make <u>canticles</u> of my cantos. The poem will please if it is lively – if it is stupid it will fail – but I will have none of your damned cutting & slashing. If you please you may publish <u>anonymously</u> it will perhaps be better; but I will battle my way against them all – like a porcupine. So you and Mr Foscolo &c want me to under-take what you call a 'great work', an epic poem I suppose or some such pyramid. I'll try no such thing – I hate tasks – and then 'seven or eight years' God send us all well this day three months – let alone years – if one's years can't be better employed than in sweating poesy – a man had better be a ditcher. And works too! – is Childe Harold nothing? You have so many '<u>divine</u>' poems – is it nothing to have written

a <u>human</u> one? Without any of your worn out machinery.
Why – man – I could have spun the thought of the four
cantos of that poem into twenty – had I wanted to book-
make – & its passion into as many modern tragedies – since
you want length you shall have enough of <u>Juan</u> for I'll make
50 cantos. And Foscolo too! Why does he not do something
more than the letters of Ortis – and a tragedy – and
pamphlets – he has a good fifteen years more at his
command than I have – what has he done all that time?
Proved his genius doubtless – but not fixed its fame – nor
done his utmost. Besides I mean to write my best work in
<u>Italian</u> – & it will take me nine years more thoroughly to
master the language – & then if my fancy exists & I exist
too – I will try what I <u>can</u> do <u>really</u>. As to the estimation of
the English which you talk of, ~~have~~ let them calculate what
it is worth – before they insult me with their insolent
condescension. I have not written for their pleasure; if they
are pleased – it is that they chose to be so, I have never flattered their opinions – nor their pride – nor will I. Neither
will I make 'Ladies books' 'al dilettar le femine e la plebe' – I
have written from the fullness of my mind, from passion –
from impulse – from many motives – but not for their
'sweet voices'. I know the precise worth of popular applause
– for few scribblers have had more – of it – and if I chose
to swerve into their paths – I could retain it or resume it –
or increase it – but I neither love ye – nor fear ye – and
though I buy with ye – and sell with ye – and talk with ye
– I will neither eat with ye – drink with ye – nor pray with
ye. They made me without my search a species of popular
idol – they – without reason or judgement beyond the
caprice of their good pleasure – threw down the image from
its pedestal – it was not broken with the fall – and they

would it seems again replace it — but they shall not. You ask about my health — about the beginning of the year — I was in a ~~great~~ state of great exhaustion — attended by such debility of stomach — ~~is~~ that nothing remained upon it — and I was obliged to reform my 'way of life' which was conducting me from the 'yellow leaf' to the ground with all deliberate speed. I am better in health and morals — and very much yours ever,

Byron

P.S. Tell Mrs [Augusta] Leigh I never had 'my Sashes' and I want some tooth-powder — the red — by all or any means.

Lord Byron

Murray wrote to Byron in 1818 admitting that 'having fired the bomb, here I am [in Wimbledon] out of the way of the explosion'. By this he was referring to the public reaction to the publication of *Don Juan* Cantos I and II. Aside from its scandalous parts, many recognised that the genius of Byron had been given free rein in the poem. One of the most articulate and insightful commentators was Murray's author, archivist and historian Francis Palgrave.

Francis Palgrave, formerly Cohen, to John Murray II, Hadlows, Kent, 16 July 1819

10 o'clock

Dear Murray

I am heartily sorry that I cannot (at least I fear that I cannot) eat my dinner at Wimbledon tomorrow; if I can dispatch a fellow with whom I have some business to transact at an early hour I will come down. Tell Mrs Murray that if she presents you with a boy, you must christen him Don Juan, & if it is a girl, why then you must call her Mazeppa!

Don Juan is an outstanding performance indeed. I am sorry that Lord B. has published it. Not that I have any right to care about principles & morality, but as an admirer of his transcendent genius I fear it will do him a mischief. Don Juan won't do any mischief, no, no mischief at all; it is a miserable piece of mock morality to cry out against such things. If a woman is inclined to be kissed otherwise than as the law directs, the devil cannot teach her more than she does know, nor can all the angels in heaven cause her to unlearn her lessons.

The sins which will be imputed to the Don are less than venial, as far as regards the effort & tendency of the work. But Lord Byron is guilty towards himself, the abuse of his wife is cruel & unmanly. The bursts and touches of poetry of a higher order are exquisite, his wit is graceful, elastic, nervous & supple. Like Shakespeare he shows that his soul can soar well into the seventh heaven, & that when he returns into this body he can be as merry as if sublimity ne'er was known. But Lord B. should have been grave & gay by turns; grave in one page & gay in the next; grave in one stanza & gay in the next; grave in one line, & gay in the next. And not grave & gay in the same page, or in the same stanza, or in the same line. If he had followed Ariosto more clearly, he would have produced a masterpiece, & not a spurt of fancy. Nothing can be better calculated to display the labours of a great poet, than a composition admitting of a ready transition from fun & frisking to sublimity & pathos, but this thing must be interchanged, they must not be mixed up together:

they must be kept distinct – though contemplated jointly. If we stand on a mountain we gladly view a storm breaking on one side of the horizon & dark clouds impending & the sun shining bright & calm in the other quarter of the heavens, but we are never drenched & scorched at the same instant whilst standing in one spot.

Don Juan must sell; grave good people, pious people, regular people, all like to read about naughty people, & even wicked words, such as I must not write, do not really offend many very modest eyes. Even D'Israeli has ~~not~~ no objection to a little innocent bawdry. Shag is a main article in the tobacconist's shop; it sells better than pig tail.

Let us have Casti by all manner of means.

Yours truly

F. C.

Parliamentarian and First Secretary of the Admiralty John Wilson Croker was a Murray's author, editor and leading contributor to the *Quarterly Review*. His diverse works included poetry, politics, biography, history and children's books, as well as editing James Boswell's *Life of Samuel Johnson* (1831). His opinions on literary matters therefore carried significant weight with Murray.

John Wilson Croker to John Murray II, Munster House, 26 March 1820

Dear Murray

I have to thank you for letting me see your two new cantos [III and IV], which I return. What sublimity! what levity! what boldness! what tenderness! what majesty! what trifling! what variety! what <u>tediousness</u>! – for tedious to a strange degree, it must be confessed that whole passages are, particularly the earlier stanzas of the fourth canto. I know no man of such general powers of intellect as Brougham, yet I think <u>him</u> insufferably tedious; and I fancy the reason to be that he has such <u>facility</u> of expression that he is never recalled to a <u>selection</u> of his thoughts. A more costive orator would be obliged to choose, and a man of his talents could not fail to choose the best; but the power of uttering all and everything which passes across his mind, tempts him to say all. He goes on without thought – I should rather say, without pause. His speeches are poor from their richness, and dull from their infinite variety. An impediment in his speech would make him a perfect Demosthenes. Something of the same kind, and with something of the same effect, is Lord Byron's wonderful fertility of thought and facility of expression; and the Protean style of 'Don Juan', instead of checking (as the fetters of rhythm generally do) his natural activity, not only gives him wider limits to range in, but even generates a more roving disposition. I dare swear, if the truth were known, that his digressions and repetitions generate one another, and that the happy jingle of some of his comical rhymes has led him on to episodes of which he never originally thought; and thus it is that, with the most extraordinary merit, merit of all kinds, these two cantos have been to <u>me</u>, in several points, tedious and even obscure.

As to the PRINCIPLES, all the world, and you, Mr Murray, <u>first of all</u>, have done this poem great injustice. There are levities here and there, more than good taste approves, but nothing to make such a terrible rout about – nothing so bad as 'Tom Jones', nor within a hundred degrees of 'Count Fathom'.

I mean some expressions of political and personal feelings

which, I believe, he, in fact, never felt, and threw in wantonly and de gaiété de coeur, and which he would have omitted, advisedly and de bonté de coeur, if he had not been goaded by indiscreet, contradictory, and urgent criticisms, which, in some cases, were dark enough to be called calumnies. But these are blowing over, if not blown over; and I cannot but think that if Mr Gifford, or some friend on whose taste and disinterestedness Lord Byron could rely, were to point out to him the cruelty to individuals, the injury to the national character, the offence to public taste, and the injury to his own reputation, of such passages as those about Southey and Waterloo and the British government and the head of that government, I cannot but hope and believe that these blemishes in the first cantos would be wiped away in the next edition; and that some that occur in the two cantos (which you sent me) would never see the light. What interest can Lord Byron have in being the poet of a party in politics? In politics, he cannot be what he appears, or rather what Messrs Hobhouse and Leigh Hunt wish to make him appear. A man of his birth, a man of his taste, a man of his talents, a man of his habits, can have nothing in common with such miserable creatures as we now call Radicals, of whom I know not that I can better express the illiterate and blind ignorance and vulgarity than by saying that the best informed of them have probably never heard of Lord Byron. No, no, Lord Byron may be indulgent to these jackal followers of his; he may connive at their use of his name – nay, it is not to be denied that he has given them too, too much countenance – but he never can, I should think, now that he sees not only the road but the rate they are going, continue to take a part so contrary to all his own interests and feelings, and to the feelings and interests of all the respectable part of his country.

But what is to be the end of all this rigmarole of mine? To
conclude, this – to advise you, for your own sake as a
tradesman, for Lord Byron's sake as a poet, for the sake of
good literature and good principles, which ought to be
united, to take such measures as you may be able to venture
upon to get Lord Byron to revise these two cantos, and not
to make another step in the odious path which Hobhouse
beckons him to pursue.

Yours ever

J. W. Croker

Following Byron's death in Greece in 1824, Murray acquired
all Byron's outstanding copyrights, including those for the *Don
Juan* cantos published by others, allowing him to bring out
numerous editions of Byron's complete works.

9

'Our ancient friendship'
The Disraelis

———•———

Isaac D'Israeli was literary adviser to both John Murray I and II who published his collections of satirical and humorous stories and essays under such titles as *Curiosities of Literature* (1791–1823), *An Essay on the Literary Character* (1795), *Calamities of Authors* (1812–13) and *Quarrels of Authors* (1814). Their families enjoyed an intimate friendship, as this letter shows.

Isaac D'Israeli to John Murray II, Bloomsbury Square, London, 12 July 1821

My Dear Friend

I have just received a magnificent present of a very beautiful writing desk; our ancient friendship required no fresh confirmation – yet I will not deny myself once more to add so considerably to those marks of kindness which your work and liberal spirit so frequently indulged.

I often think of you, my dear friend, without any other object of suggestion than the zealous wishes for your welfare – your happiness – your good name and celebrity you have secured, and now have only to guard.

My son Benjamin is quite delighted and proud of the valuable and elegant volume you have with so much taste presented him.

I hope we shall see you at Tunbridge Wells – choose only fair weather and come as soon, and as often as you can find amusement.

All here unite in best regards; and believe me, most sincerely

Yours I.

If Mrs Murray does not receive a letter this morning she will in a day or two, with necessary particulars about Wimbledon.

However, the families were to fall out over John Murray II's attempt to establish the *Representative* as a rival to *The Times* newspaper. The project involved Isaac's twenty-one-year-old son Benjamin, who would later go on to fame as a writer and politician, yet Benjamin's ambitions as a newspaper editor were not matched by his talents in other fields. Sent by Murray to Scotland to gain the support of Walter Scott and his son-in-law John Gibson Lockhart for the paper, Disraeli decided that secrecy and code-names were necessary in his correspondence so that advance notice of their involvement would not become public. Murray subsequently annotated the letter in an attempt to identify Scott, Lockhart, senior Tory politician George Canning and Permanent Secretary to the Admiralty Sir John Barrow. 'O For the political Puck' is perhaps Disraeli himself.

Benjamin Disraeli to John Murray II, Edinburgh, 18 September 1825

My Dear Sir

I sent a dispatch by Saturdays night's post directed to Mr Barrow – You have doubtless received it safe – As I consider

you are anxious to hear minutely of the state of my operation I again send you a few lines. I receive I received this
morning a very polite letter from L. He had just received
that morning (Saturday) Wright's letter – I enclose you copy
of L.'s letter, as it will be interesting to you to see or judge
what effect was produced on his mind by its perusal – I
have written today to say that I will call at Chiefswood on
Tuesday – I intend to go to Melrose tomorrow, but as I will
not take the chance of meeting him the least tired I shall
sleep at Melrose and call on the following morning.

I shall of course accept his offer of staying there. I shall
call again at B.'s before my departure tomorrow to see if
there is any dispatch from you – You will judge whether in
future it will be more expedient to send to B. or to Mr L.'s.
The first one will prevent the franker suspecting the object
of my visit – but on the other hand will make your letters
come at least a day later – I shall give B. my direction to
forward in case you send.

I shall continue to give you advices of all my movements.
You will agree with me that I have at least not lost any time,
but that all things have gone very well as yet.

There is of course no danger in our communications of
anything unfairly transpiring – but from the very delicate
nature of names interested, it will be expedient to adopt
some cloak.

The Chevalier will speak for itself [Sir W. S.]
M – from Melrose – for Mr L. [-ockhart]
X for a certain personage on whom we called one
    day – who lives a slight distance from town, and
    who was then unwell – [Canning]
O For the political Puck.

Mr Chronometer will speak for itself, at least to all
those who give African dinners. [J. M. Barrow?]

I think this necessary; & try to remember it.

I am quite delighted with Edinburg. Its beauties become
every moment more – apparent – The view from the Calton
Hill finds me a frequent votary –

In the present state of affairs I suppose it will not be
expedient to leave the letter for Mr Bruce – It will seem
odd p.p.c. [to take leave]with at the same moment I bring a
letter of introduction – If I return to Ed. I can avail myself
of it – If the letter contains anything which would otherwise
make Mr Murray wish it to be left, let me know – Read
my letters & write to me – I revel in the various beauties of
a Scotch breakfast – gol cold grouse & marmalade find me
however constant –

Ever yours
B. D.

The *Representative* was published only between January and July
1826 and its failure cost Murray around £26,000: a huge amount
of money – enough to buy No. 50 six times over. The families
unfortunately fell out, with Mrs D'Israeli writing: 'I really cannot
believe John Murray who has so often professed such strong
friendship for D'Israeli should be now going about blasting the
character of that friend's son because he had formed in his
versatile imagination a perfect being and expected impossibilities and found him on trial a mere mortal and a very young
man. I fear I have made this letter too long and that you will
destroy it instead of reading it, pray for old friendship do not
do that but give me the explanation I so ardently require.'

Despite this plea for reconciliation Benjamin Disraeli

lampooned Murray in his novel *Vivian Grey* (1826–7), but in 1832 Murray's published his *Contarini Fleming* which, despite the author considering it his best work, was a financial disappointment; author and publisher shared a modest £36 profit.

10

'The value of works of imagination
it is impossible to predict'
William Wordsworth

⸺⸺◆⸺⸺

The poet William Wordsworth had difficult relationships with publishers. Although initially prolific he often laboured over his writing before having the confidence to publish. His earliest published works in 1793 were followed by his first major volume, *Lyrical Ballads* (1798), as a joint publication with Samuel Taylor Coleridge. While half a dozen books followed up to *Peter Bell* (1819) his only major poem afterwards was *The Prelude* (1850), published shortly after his death.

In 1825, dissatisfied with his then publisher, he asked his friend and fellow poet Robert Southey 'whether there be in the trade more liberality, more enterprize, or more skill in managing the sale of works charactered and circumstanced as mine are, than have fallen to the lot of Messrs Longman & Co'. Southey recommended his own publisher, Murray's, and agreed to act as an intermediary. This was not an easy task as Wordsworth distrusted all publishers, stating he would not be 'dependent upon their countenance, consideration, patronage, or by whatever term they may dignify their ostentation or selfish vanity'. This certainly applied to John Murray II whom he considered had the 'airs of a patron'. When negotiations first via Southey and then by Samuel Rogers, another Romantic poet, showed little progress, Wordsworth decided to write directly to Murray himself.

William Wordsworth to John Murray II, Rydal Mount near
Kendal, 6 August 1825

Dear Sir

Upwards of 3 months ago I think, in consequence of a
letter from Mr Rogers expressing the terms upon which you
would print 750 copies of my Poems in 6 vols., I wrote to
beg you would inform me what would be the cost &c, as
without that knowledge I would not close the bargain.
Having waited so long for your answer, I conclude it is not
convenient for you to enter upon this undertaking; & therefore feel myself at liberty to make other arrangements if an
opportunity should occur.

Some time ago I was much concerned to hear thro' Mr
Southey that you had been unwell but were then recovered:
had it not been for this indisposition, I should have written
to you sooner.

I remain, Dear Sir
Faithfully yours
Wm Wordsworth

This letter did not elicit the response Wordsworth craved so
he wrote in frustration to Rogers on 15 August 1825: 'Month
after month elapses and I receive no answer from the grand
Murray. I will not pay him the compt. to say I am offended
at this . . . I am persuaded that he is too great a personage for
anyone but a court, an aristocratic or most fashionable author
to deal with. You will recollect the time that elapsed before
you could bring him to terms – for the pains you then took
I thank you again.'

Wordsworth then asked another literary friend, Alaric Watts,
to negotiate a deal with publishers Robinson and Hurst. These

discussions also collapsed as a result of an offer Wordsworth thought too low. He flirted again with Longman's, but also re-approached Murray, who consulted his literary adviser John Gibson Lockhart. He gave a considered reply, as well as a commentary on Percy Bysshe Shelley's poetry.

John Gibson Lockhart to John Murray II, London, 9 July 1826

Dear Murray

I should have sooner acknowledged your letter enclosing cheques for the Review. But I thought I have had some other matters to write about ere now. I shall probably hear the result of your conference to Dr S. tomorrow.

In regard to Wordsworth I certainly cannot doubt that it must be creditable to any publisher to publish the works of one who is and must continue to be a classic poet of England. Your adventure with [George] Crabbe, however, ought to be a lesson of much caution. On the other hand, again, W.'s poems <u>must</u> become more popular, else why so many editions in the course of the last few years. There have been <u>two</u> of the Excursion alone and I know that those have not satisfied the public. Everything, I should humbly say, depends on the terms proposed by the great Laker, whose vanity, be it whispered, is nearly as remarkable as his genius.

I have Shelley's posthumous vol. in Pall Mall. It would be easy to make a charming vol. of 'Beauties' – but a small one it must be. By far the least of his original works 'The Cenci' is shocking for its subject – the incest of a father & a daughter. The task of selection would be a difficult & a debatable one. I should for the sake of Shelley's genius rejoice & see it done: but I doubt whether the father has

the power to authorise it – Shelley left children I think &
I know not but the mother may be the person – who of
course would think the most immoral & irreligious
productions the best & scorn the notion of castration
literary almost as thoroughly as she would the physical
operation.

Yours sincerely

J. G. Lockhart

Lockhart's references to Murray's too liberal payment (an enormous advance of £3,000) and loss with George Crabbe's poems
and Wordsworth's vanity made Murray pause. When negotiations
were taken up again Wordsworth set out in detail the publishing
terms he expected.

*William Wordsworth to John Murray II, Rydal Mount, near
Ambleside, 4 December 1826*

Dear Sir

I have at last determined to go to the press with my
Poems as early as possible. Twelve months ago they were to
have been put into the hands of Messrs Robinson and Hurst,
upon the terms of payment of a certain sum independent of
expense on my part, but the failure of that house prevented
the thing going forward.

Before I offer the publication to anyone but yourself
upon the <u>different</u> principle agreed on between you and me,
as you may recollect, viz the author to meet two-thirds of
the expenses & risk, and to share two-thirds of the profit, I
think it proper to <u>renew</u> that proposal to you.

If you are not inclined to accept it, I shall infer so from
your silence, if such an arrangement suits you pray let me

immediately know, and all I have to request is, that without
loss of time, when I have informed you of the intended
quantity of letter press, you will then let me know what my
share of the expense will amount to –

I am, Dear Sir
Your obedient servant
Wm Wordsworth

As Murray did not answer promptly, Wordsworth assumed he
was uninterested, and yet another literary representative became
involved, Henry Crabb Robinson, who called upon Murray
on 25 January 1827 to receive his decision. He afterwards
reported to Wordsworth that Murray had confessed himself
'shamefully inattentive' to the recent proposals and that he was
'happy to publish his works on his own terms'.

In 1827 Longman brought out the collected edition of
Wordsworth's poems, to modest success. Later editions helped
build Wordsworth's reputation and popularity, and he eventually
succeeded his friend Southey as Poet Laureate in 1843. Murray,
although never Wordsworth's publisher, played a part in this
success by publishing supportive reviews of his poetry by Henry
Taylor in the *Quarterly Review* in 1834 and 1841, for which
Wordsworth sent this grudging acknowledgement.

William Wordsworth to John Murray II, Rydal Mount, near
Ambleside, 2 December 1834

Mr Wordsworth presents his compts to Mr Murray – &
thanks him for the present of the Quarterly Review which
was duly received. The notice of Mr W.'s Poems is written
with candour & generous praise – which whether just or
not will doubtless promote the interests of true taste, by

assisting in the circulation of Poems whose <u>faults</u>, whatever they may be, are not of a class that in this age is likely to be imitated.

[unsigned]

11

'It will add greatly to the popularity of the work' On Illustration

———•———

Scottish explorer Sir Alexander Burnes's success as a spy and in undertaking secret surveying work in north-west India and Afghanistan was thanks both to his faculty for languages and the fact that he adopted native dress. His letters from exotic locations were always full of interest and intrigue.

Alexander Burnes to John Murray II, The Nile River, Egypt, 20 March 1835

My Dear Murray

It is only four weeks this very day since I took leave of you in Albemarle Street, and here I am within a couple of hours' sail of Grand Cairo and in sight of those stupendous monuments of folly, the Pyramids of Egypt, which as my favourite author Gibbon has put it 'still stand erect and unshaken above the floods of the Nile, after an hundred generations and the leaves of autumn have dropped into the grave.' I cannot believe myself so far distant from the salons of London, but the moment I reached Alexandria the line of demarcation was too apparent, the transition from civilization to barbarism was instantaneous, and we received before quitting the steamer the astounding intelligence that 15,000 human beings had died of plague within the last

three months, and that 129 had perished on the preceding
day in the isolated town of Alexandria. My fellow passengers
and myself tumbled our boxes into a boat and set off for
Cairo without holding conversation with a human being
and hitherto our journey has been most prosperous – a
couple of days more will transport us across the Isthmus,
and we shall in all probability reach India within fifty days
of quitting the Land's End. What locomotion! Before I have
done with it I shall begin to doubt my existence; as it is, I
do take these towering masses, which they all tell me are
the Pyramids, for those beautiful lithographs which I was
looking at with Mrs Murray on your table a month since,
but then I have since spanned a goodly portion of the
world, and, as you expressed some interest in my wander-
ings, I have resolved to fill this sheet by telling you what
you and your friends may expect who are resolved on
profiting by this new steam communication with India and
what you may do in three months . . .

Having thus landed in Egypt in twenty-two days, a
month, or rather six weeks, may be spent in visiting Cairo,
Jerusalem, Damascus, and by availing myself of the packet
after the next it would be quite possible to be in London in
three months! One author – I forget his name – gives his
book the name of 'Dates and Distances, showing what may
be done', &c. in a certain time. He does not outdo this,
which ought to tempt some of the thousand and one tourists who wish to write a 'book for next season', and sigh for
immortality as authors.

The Quarterly is lying before me and, strange enough, I
have been reperusing the very article which treats of
Mahommed Ali in that able essay regarding the encroach-
ment of Russia. The journal from which the quotations are

made regarding the state and government of Egypt proves the writer to have been an accurate and an acute observer, but I do think that he has been too severe on the Pasha. To be sure he is a wholesale merchant and a wholesale oppressor, but compare him with his predecessors in this land of bondsmen, and then judge. From the very spot where I first beheld the Pyramids, Mahommed Ali has begun to dig an enormous aqueduct into which he is to turn the Nile after having bridged a new channel! The bridge is to be so constructed that he may inundate any part above the delta, and the river itself will be passed out of its channel by an embankment which is to be formed by boats filled with stones and sunk across it! Is this the work of a barbarian? Can a work so useful, though he may force the peasants to perform it, be called anything but a national undertaking, and whence are the supplies to be derived by Mahommed Ali but from his 'faithful Commons'? But I must be done: Cairo is in sight, the boatmen are singing a song of delight, in the music not such, however, as attended Cleopatra in her galley, nor enough to make me charmed into a forgetfulness of all your many attentions to me. With the best regards to Mrs Murray and your family, and particular remembrances to your son.

Ever believe me,

Yours very sincerely,

Alex Burnes

P.S. I go to the Pyramids tomorrow morning, and start in the evening for the Red Sea: quick work – but not too quick – for 190 people died here (Cairo) yesterday of the plague.

A. B.

Burnes's travels made him a hero, gaining a royal audience, a knighthood, the gold medal of the Royal Geographical Society, fellowship of the Royal Society and honorary membership of the Royal Asiatic Society. For his *Travels into Bokhara; being the account of a journey from India to Cabool, Tartary, and Persia* (1834) John Murray II commissioned Daniel Maclise to paint Burnes's portrait dressed in native Afghan costume and a turban, suggesting to Burnes that the likeness be engraved as the book's frontispiece. He agreed as long as it be titled '"The Costume of Bokhara". It will then be known that it is a portrait & will save me from the appearance of vanity.' When the book was advertised without this clarification he wrote to Murray.

Alexander Burnes to John Murray II, 13 June 1834

My Dear Sir

I see the advertisement in the Quarterly states my book to be accompanied by a 'portrait of the author' – You would oblige me very much by altering this in the subsequent advertisements i.e. leaving it out, for the portrait is engraved as the 'Costume of Bokhara' & it was intended to have the knowing ones to find it out –

Believe me

Very truly yours

Alex Burnes

Burnes wrote again to Murray on 28 December 1834: 'if you could make some alteration in <u>my visage</u> in the "Costume of Bokhara" for it is said to be so arch and cunning that I shall be handed down to posterity as a real Tartar!! Suppose you strike it out altogether or get Mr Maclise to touch it up a little, or suppose you substitute a lithograph of the miniature I showed to you & which my brother has. Do any of the three which you like.' Murray paid the engraver Edward Finden to alter the portrait for subsequent editions.

Murray worked regularly with the great artist Joseph Mallord William Turner, including commissions for the *Life and Works of Lord Byron* (1833–4) and his joint publication, with Charles Tilt, of Finden's *Landscape Illustrations of the Bible* (1833–6). To assist Turner and the other artists, including Augustus Wall Callcott, they were given drawings made at the relevant locations. The architect Charles Barry, who had toured Greece, the

Balkans and the Holy Land in 1817–20, supplied numerous sketches, although he became frustrated with the inaccuracy of the artists' interpretations of his work.

Charles Barry to John Murray III, Foley Place, London,
28 January 1833

My Dear Sir

Many thanks for the loan of Wood's work and the Quarterly Review. I have seen Turner's drawings at Finden's this morning – they are certainly very beautiful as works of art but there are some anomalies about them such as the sun & moon being in the valley together and in the southern view of Jerusalem the sun in full splendour <u>in the</u> <u>north</u> – I intend to call upon the tickleish gentleman and see whether I can induce him to correct these and some other trifling departures from fidelity by which the character of the country suffers. I have forwarded by your man to him and Callcott their respective portfolios with lists of the sketches they contain & I will send to you tomorrow morning copies of those lists in which you will find blanks left for filling up with quotations and other illustrative memoranda.

Yours very truly
Charles Barry

It was a challenging job for William and Edward Finden, the leading engravers of their day, to keep the egos of the artists and the demands of the publishers in balance. In this letter they solicited Murray's intervention with Callcott who felt harassed by them.

W. & E. Finden to John Murray II, Southampton Place, London, 14 January 1833

My Dear Sir

Enclosed you will find a proof of the woodcut intended for the cover, how do you like it? We shall be glad to hear.

We take the opportunity of writing to you upon a subject that still occupies our thoughts: it is <u>this</u>. As it never was the intention, or wish, of either my brother or myself to give offence to Mr Callcott, and as we believe that he is in some measure convinced that such is the fact. We have been thinking that (as you are in communication with that gentleman) it might be possible to shew him that we are still anxious to avail ourselves of his talents in the book, and avoid the <u>publicity</u> of any <u>breach</u> by requesting him to make some drawings <u>occasionally</u> as his <u>convenience</u> would allow him. There would be no difficulty about the sketches as he might select any of those that he has the direct means of procuring.

We think this would be of advantage to all parties, and we submit it to your consideration to adopt, or reject, as it may appear on reflection to be advisable, or not.

We are
Dear Sir
Your obliged servants
W. & E. Finden

Murray was able to mediate between artist and engravers with the help of his friend Maria Graham, who had married Augustus Callcott in 1827. She played an important, but largely unacknowledged, role in preparing sources for the illustrations and writing on behalf of her husband as the tension increased.

Maria Callcott, née Graham, to John Murray II, Kensington Gravel Pitts, 30 September 1833

My Dear Sir

I have persuaded Mr Callcott (& indeed he was not very unwilling) to let me send you the accompanying letters which have passed between him & the Messrs Findens relative to the Bible illustrations. In your son's absence Mr Callcott cannot but feel it just both to him & to you, to shew how his name has been used as a party to a proceeding that nothing can persuade us he would have authorised.

When Mr Callcott first overcame his extreme reluctance to enter into any engagement with the Messrs Findens for either the Byron illustrations or the Bible work, it was principally because he respected <u>you</u> and remembered with very grateful feelings your long friendship for & kindness to me. And even now in withdrawing from the work on account of Messrs Findens' unhandsome proceedings, he feels for <u>your</u> sake so much interest in it, that he is determined on giving whatever assistance may be farther in his or my power as to procuring subjects &c – I learned only two days ago that some drawings I had requested to have made in the most interesting part of lower Egypt would be done expertly for us – & my friend Mrs C. Bracebridge will bring sketches with her from Palestine which I have no doubt will be useful as I gave her a list of the things most wanted. These – should I live till they arrive – I shall have the pleasure of forwarding to your son myself – otherwise I know that Mr Callcott will do so. Make my kindest remembrances to Mrs Murray & your daughters and believe me, My Dear Sir

Yours very faithfully

Maria Callcott

P.S. I ought to congratulate you on your son's escape from the precipices of St Gothard.

John Murray III was a keen Alpinist. It is not known what untoward event occurred in 1833, but it did not put him off returning to the St Gotthard Pass in 1855, when he fell off a narrow path in the dark over a 1,200-foot precipice. Fortunately, he landed on a ledge only twelve feet down, but was knocked unconscious before he was rescued.

Murray's tradition of working with distinguished illustrators was maintained into the next century. Kathleen Hale wrote and illustrated nineteen *Orlando the Marmalade Cat* children's books between 1938 and 1972, including *Orlando the Judge* (1950) and *Orlando the Marmalade Cat Goes to the Moon* (1968) – a year before Neil Armstrong made it there. To ensure the quality of the illustrations she made her own lithographic plates and reckoned that each book 'took four to five months of working seven hours a day, seven days a week'. Her amusing letters to Murray were sometimes humorously illustrated.

Kathleen Hale to John Murray VI, May 1950

The lithography is finished, likewise the lithographer.
K. Hale

Kathleen Hale to John Murray VI, 6 May 1968

My Dear Jock

Just to let you know that Orlando is on his last lap & should be Home & Dry in about 10 days.

Love from
Kathleen

Katherine Tozer's children's book character Mumfie, the little elephant, often added postscripts to her mummy's (creator's) letters. Often these thanked Jock Murray for his gifts of sweets. In this case Mumfie sent this letter herself, enclosing Jock's Christmas present.

Mumfie to John Murray VI, 1940

HOME. WENZDAI

DEAR UNCL JON

I AM ZENDING YOO
SUM OF YOR FAVRIT
CIGRETTZ FOR XMURS
PLEEZ DONT TEL MI
MA BECOZ SHE SES
THEY AR NORST NORS-
YATING. I HOPE YOO
GETZ LOTS IN YOR

2

STOKING

LUV FROM
MUMFIE XXX

P.Z. I HAV LURNT
HOW TO SPEL
UNCL RITE
P.S. THIZ IS MY
MA'S INK.

These jocular letters were to come to a tragic end when Katherine died giving birth to her son Hamish. Her husband Jim sent Jock Murray this poignant postcard, originally intended to convey joyful news but instead giving a heartbreaking message.

Robert James 'Jim' McCallum Tozer, Cold Harbour, Chiddingfold,
Surrey, 6 August 1943

John dear, This postcard was to let you know that Hamish
arrived this morning but my darling left me this afternoon
suddenly. Bless you for always being so sweet to her.

Jim

The following illustration was given to Jock Murray by Beryl
Cook who was much amused to hear that her saucy jacket for
The Works (1978) had been banned and removed in Ireland.
The idea for this illustration came to her after she met John
Betjeman at No. 50.

Archibald - shielding Jumbo's
eyes from the sight of my
book.

Sir John Betjeman to John Murray VI, Radnor Walk, London,
8 December 1978

Dear Jock

I am so overjoyed with Beryl Cook's drawing with
Jumbo having his eyes shielded from The Works that I want
another copy of it – I am sticking to the one you sent me.
It is the best book you have published for years and I would
like to think of your uncle in Heaven reading it.

I think the new Dean of St Paul's [Alan Webster] is a
very nice man. His son Stephen is a poet. The new Dean is
too unworldly for the City and that is a good thing. He
saved many Norwich churches from destruction. Love to
Diana, John R. and so on to Nicholas Perren.

Yours sincerely,

JB

12

Sartor Resartus
Thomas Carlyle

———◆———

Generally regarded as one of his greatest works and a classic of English literature, the philosopher Thomas Carlyle's novel *Sartor Resartus* (the tailor re-tailored) was serialised in *Fraser's Magazine* (1833–4) and published in book form in America in 1836, but his first attempt to have the work published was years before with Murray's. He travelled from Craigenputtock, his Scottish farm, to London to find a publisher and, on the recommendation of Francis Jeffrey, judge, literary critic and editor of the *Edinburgh Review*, Carlyle first tried Murray's.

Thomas Carlyle to John Murray II, Woburn Buildings, Tavistock Square, London, 10 August 1831

Dear Sir

I here send you the MS; concerning which I have, for the present, only to repeat my urgent request that no time may be lost in deciding on it. At latest next Wednesday I shall wait upon you, to see what farther, or whether anything farther, is to be done.

In the meanwhile, it is perhaps unnecessary to say that the whole business is <u>strictly confidential</u>; the rather as I wish to publish anonymously.

I remain

Dear Sir

Yours truly

Thomas Carlyle

Be so kind as write by the bearer these two words: 'MS received.'

Carlyle became increasingly frustrated by Murray's delay and visited Murray on 17 August, noting to his wife Jane: 'The dog of a bookseller gone to the country. I leave my card with remonstrances and pressing enquiries <u>when</u>. The clerk talks of "Mr Murray writing you, sir"; I will call again tomorrow morning and make M. speak to me, I hope.' The following week he returned and complained that 'Murray as usual was not in; but an answer lay for me: my poor Teufelsdreck wrapped in new paper, with a letter stuck under the pack thread! I took with a silent fury, and walked off. The letter said, he regretted exceedingly &c that – all his literary friends were out of town, he himself occupied with a sick family in the country; that he had conceived the finest hopes &c; in short that Teufelsdreck had never been looked into; but that if I would let him keep it for a month, he would <u>then</u> be able to say a word, and by God's blessing a favourable one.'

Carlyle then consulted other publishers but with little success, making him conclude that 'Murray is clearly the man, if he <u>will</u>: only I have <u>lost</u> ten days by him already; for he might have told me what he did finally tell in one day. It is said, he drinks a little liberally.'

Eventually Murray agreed to publish, but Carlyle decided to see if another publisher might make a better offer. When Murray discovered this, he wrote on 17 September: 'Under these circumstances it will be necessary for me also to get it read by some literary friend, before I can, in justice to myself, engage in the printing of it.' The friend in question was the Reverend Henry Hart Milman, who sent this opinion.

Reverend Henry Hart Milman to John Murray II, Pinner Grove, Middlesex, 4 October 1831

My Dear Sir

I have read Mr Carlisle's MS. He is a very clever man, completely Germanised in thought and even in language. To me who am familiar with the terms of German philosophy and the manner in which those writers think and express themselves, the work was very amusing, but I doubt whether the English public will enter into it – the wit as well as the rest is German, and though occasionally very clever, is perhaps more often strange and fantastic. It is really a pity that so much cleverness and knowledge should be wasted; and about such works the taste of the public is so whimsical that it is not easy to anticipate their verdict, but still I cannot conceive that they will on the whole either understand or what is worse have the patience with the length of what ought to have been a short and lively jeu d'esprit – Though it is still more German for being so elaborate – the want of liveliness and rapidity will hardly be endured by our impatient taste. It is rather like the worthy German who was found jumping over the chairs and tables 'pour apprendre s'estre vif' – After all is it a translation or original – for you have not sent the first sheets.

Believe me, My Dear Sir

Ever truly yours

H. H. Milman

I expect to be in town on <u>Thursday</u>.

Milman's criticism with Murray's rejection of the manuscript were forwarded to Carlyle, whose wife Jane wrote to Carlyle's mother, on 6 October: 'They are not going to print the book after all – Murray has lost heart lest it do not take with the public and so like a stupid ass, as he is, has sent the manuscript back.'

13

'A Life of Adventures'
Byron's Life and Letters

After Lord Byron's death in Greece in 1824, aged thirty-six, his family and literary executors decided that his memoirs, which he had intended Murray's to publish, should instead be burned. This was done in Murray's fireplace at 50 Albemarle Street and is often cited as one of the most heinous acts of literary vandalism. At the time, however, John Murray II was praised for acting in a gentlemanly fashion, sacrificing his own publishing interests in deference to the family's sensitivities. Byron's friend Thomas Moore had been appointed his posthumous editor, a role he maintained thanks to Byron's still extensive surviving archives. He edited for publication a two-volume *The Letters and Journals of Lord Byron: With notices of his life* (1830) which was hugely profitable. This marked the beginning of Murray's two-centuries-long publishing association with Byron biographies and editions of his letters, in which they always defended his reputation, despite its many ups and downs.

❖❖❖❖❖❖

Byron's most frequent correspondent was Murray himself, and it was these letters that Moore found the most shocking. He wrote on one occasion that 'Murray showed me a letter which Lord Byron had written him, which is to me unaccountable, except from the most ungovernable vanity – He there details to him (to Murray, the bookseller – a person so out of his caste & to whom he writes formally, beginning "Dear Sir") the details of an intrigue in which he says he is at this very moment actually engaged with a Venetian girl . . . for the edification of Mr Murray and all the visitors to his shop – to whom it is, of course, intended he shall read the gazette of my lord's last Venetian victory – this is really too gross.' When editing Byron's letters Moore decided to be more tactful concerning Murray.

Thomas Moore to John Murray III, 10 October 1830

Dear John

I think the portrait very good, indeed, and so you may tell W. Finden. The likeness is even an improvement on the picture. I wish to send your father's criticism & proof of the Preface which I now forward to Davison – It was quite necessary to account for what, at first blush, I find startles everybody – namely, that Lord Byron should address letters upon matters so little connected with literature to his publisher. It was also my wish to enhance the value of the letters we give by showing that he wrote but little (which is the fact) to anyone else. These two points I think have gained & without saying anything, I should hope, on the <u>first</u>, that your father will dislike. It is a constant remark (which neither you nor he, of course, are likely to hear): 'How strange that a noble man should write such letters to his bookseller!' – and I think I have given what I think the true as well as most polite solution of it.

Ever yours

T. Moore

The framed print will be very welcome.

John Murray III attached a note to this letter: 'Noble man and his bookseller! End of letter. Autres temps autres mœurs.'

John Murray II sent a copy of the first of the two volumes of Moore's *Letters and Journals of Lord Byron* to the author Mary Shelley who was very appreciative of this gift.

Mary Wollstonecraft Shelley, née Godwin, to John Murray II, 19 January 1830

Except the occupation of one or two annoyances, I have done nothing but read, since I got 'Lord Byron's Life'. I have no pretensions to being a critic, yet I know infinitely well what pleases me. Not to mention the judicious arrangement and happy <u>tact</u> displayed by Mr Moore, which distinguish the book, I must say a word concerning the style, which is elegant and forcible. I was particularly struck by the observations on Lord Byron's character before his departure to Greece, and on his return. There is strength and richness, as well as sweetness.

The great charm of the work to me, and it will have the same to you, is that the Lord Byron I find there is <u>our</u> Lord Byron – the fascinating, faulty, philosophical being – daring the world, docile to a private circle, impetuous and indolent, gloomy, and yet more gay than any other. I live with him again in these pages – getting reconciled (as I used in his lifetime) to those waywardnesses which annoyed me when he was away, through the delightful tone of his conversation and manners.

His own letters and journals mirror himself as he was, and are invaluable. There is something cruelly kind in this single volume. When will the next come? Impatient before, how tenfold more so am I now. Among its many other virtues, this book is accurate to a miracle. I have not stumbled on one mistake with regard either to time, place, or feeling.

I am, Dear Sir
Your obedient and obliged servant
Mary Shelley

Mary Somerville, Scottish author of books on science and mathematics, was another to acknowledge and discuss the merits of Moore's *Life of Byron*.

Mary Somerville to John Murray II, Royal Hospital Chelsea, London, 13 January 1831

My Dear Sir

You have kindly afforded me a source of very great interest and pleasure in the perusal of the second volume of Moore's 'Life of Byron'. In my opinion, it is very superior to the first; there is less repetition of the letters; they are better written, abound more in criticism and observation, and make the reader better acquainted with Lord Byron's principles and character. His morality was certainly more suited to the meridian of Italy than England; but with all his faults there is a charm about him that excites the deepest interest and admiration. His letter to Lady Byron is more affecting and beautiful than anything I have read; it must ever be a subject of regret that it was not sent; it seems impossible that it should not have made a lasting impression, and might possibly have changed the destinies of both. With kind remembrances to Mrs Murray and the young people,

Believe me
Truly yours
Mary Somerville

Leading Conservative politician and former Prime Minister Robert Peel was delighted by his publisher Murray's gift of a one-volume edition of *The Works of Lord Byron* (1837) with its dedication by Murray to Byron's 'school- and form-fellow'.

Sir Robert Peel to John Murray II, Whitehall, London, 18 April 1837

My Dear Sir

I am much flattered by the compliment which you have paid to me in dedicating to me a beautiful edition of the works of my distinguished 'school- and form-fellow'.

I was the next boy to Lord Byron at Harrow for three or four years, and was always on very friendly terms with him, though not living in particular intimacy out of school.

I do not recollect ever having a single angry word with him, or that there ever was any the slightest jealousy or coldness between us.

It is a gratification to me to have my name associated with his in the manner in which you have placed it in friendly connection; and I do not believe, if he could have foreseen, when we were boys together at school, this con-tinuance of a sort of amicable relation between us after his death, the idea would have been otherwise than pleasing to him.

Believe me
My Dear Sir
Very faithfully yours
Robert Peel

A century after his death, Byron still continued to fascinate readers, including Charles Gibbs-Smith, a schoolboy who would go on to become a distinguished historian of aviation.

Charles Harvard Gibbs-Smith to John Murray V, Petersham Terrace, London, 15 October 1925

Dear Sir

Please receive the most grateful thanks of a mere schoolboy, for all the trouble you took. I am a great admirer of Byron from his poetry to his life and personality. However many faults he may have had he would never have been the Real Byron without them.

With great thanks
Yours sincerely
C. H. Gibbs-Smith

John Murray VI hoped to solicit a review of Doris Langley Moore's *Ada, Countess of Lovelace: Byron's legitimate daughter* (1977) from Rebecca West, a critic he greatly admired, so to learn that she did not enjoy Byron's work must have come as something of a surprise.

Rebecca West to John Murray VI, Kingston House North, London,
8 August 1977

My Dear Jock

Thank you for Ada. But I must write a letter which is
quite dreadful considering the name of the addressee and
his address! I am a heretic about Byron. I think him one
of the worst bores in the world. All his poems sound to
me as if they have been ground out on a barrel organ,
including Don Juan, which is about as good as Clive Juan,
and all his letters are surely twaddle. He got less out of
Venice than anybody before or since. Caroline Lamb and
Lady Byron were just what he deserved – and all his love
affairs seem to me as alluring as, say, John Fistein. I regard
you as the most elegant of publishers and Doris Langley
Moore as one of our most capable and really respectable
(in its proper sense) women of letters, but oh, dear, how I
wish you were not preoccupied with that patch of ground
on which the sun will never, so far as I'm concerned, cast
a ray.

I expect I will review it, but I will probably grieve you
and Mrs Langley Moore, and I apologise for it in advance.
I can't leave it alone for my mind is perpetually attracted
by the names on the pages – I wonder if poor Ada ever
had an interview with Sir David Brewster. He was neigh-
bour of my Henry's Scottish grandfather or great-
grandfather, I can't remember which, and his extreme
acerbity has become a legend in the family. I hope he
didn't see poor Ada.

With many thanks for your gift and your pleasant letter,
which is characteristic in the trouble you take to include in

it the pleasant news that Professor Wolfe liked my review of his little tome.

My blessings to you both

Rebecca

Jock Murray replied, on 11 August 1977, that he had a 'confession, to be kept to yourself – I also get stuck in the poetry!' However, he defended the letters, because 'they fascinate me in their spontaneity and in their direct (and indirect) revelation of character, whether or not that is agreeable'.

14

'This lady is the Byron of our Modern Poetesses'
Caroline Norton

———◆———

Caroline Norton, granddaughter of the playwright Richard Brinsley Sheridan, was one of the most dedicated social reformers of the nineteenth century. Having suffered in a violent marriage, she left her husband George, a barrister and MP, who then falsely accused her of an affair with Lord Melbourne and used his legal rights to separate her from their three sons. Devastated by this, she passionately and successfully campaigned for fairer social laws, especially for women in marriage and the rights of children. Her efforts helped introduce the 1839 Infant Custody Act, but her husband cynically responded by moving to Scotland where the law did not apply.

Murray's published her poem, *A Voice From the Factories* (1836), which highlighted, in realistic and harrowing detail, the plight of working-class children who laboured under awful conditions in industrial factories. She regretted having published it anonymously and, four years later, tried to persuade Murray to republish it under her own name

Caroline Norton, née Sheridan, afterwards Lady Stirling Maxwell, to John Murray II, Bolton Street, London, 15 April 1840

Dear Sir

I am about to ask an odd favour, but I am very anxious

about it. I am printing, and I am also re-<u>printing</u>; that is, I am adding to my present attempt such of my former ones as it may seem <u>worth while</u> to add.

You published for me a poem called A Voice from the Factories — anonymously — which perhaps was a mistake, for my friends knew me without my name, & those who would have bought it, for the name alone, did not know it. I am fond of the poem, & if you would allow me to reprint it, you would do me a great service, for I am in many troubles & difficulties from which I look to my poem to extricate me, as the soldier trusts to his sword to cut his way through. Of course my request is not so saucy as to expect acquiescence, except upon the ground of probability that the sale for my woman's poetry on a polit-ical subject, is come to a close — if you think otherwise, I should much wish there could be a transfer of the copy-right, as a matter of business, to my most bargaining publisher, as I wish to make my volume as complete as possible, hoping under your guidance henceforward to forsake <u>poetry</u> for <u>prose</u>. You know you hinted to me that the door of your Review would open to me, if I thought I could write for it.

I leave town on Monday; if I could hear from you before that time it would be a favour.

Yours, Dear Sir

Very truly

Caroline Norton

Murray was a staunch defender and supporter of Norton. Writing, publishing and Murray's support were of great solace to her when she felt under attack. In thanking Murray for his gift of Lord Jocelyn's *Six Months with the Chinese Expedition* (1841), Caroline wrote this amusing celebration of all things bibliographic, including Catherine Gore's *Cecil: Or, the Adventures of a coxcomb* (1841).

Caroline Norton to John Murray II, Bolton Street,
4 March 1841

Dear Sir

Thanks for Lord Jocelyn's book, which, just now that we are all gaping for Chinese information is very acceptable – and especially to <u>me</u>, who am too ill to go out & gossip with the rest of the world, and depend on the 'dumb oracles' I find in type.

Blessed be he who invented letters, Cadmus, as I was early taught.

Blessed be he who invented printing, whose name at the moment I forget.

Blessed be all the engravers, printers, designers, lithographers, facsimile copiers & makers of steel plates!

Blessed even beyond these, be all publishers, & especially those who send me copies of new books!

Blessed be authors & authoresses – but in a minor degree – a sort of beggarly blessing, such as mocked poor Esau when he wept for one, having <u>sold his birthright</u>.

Blessed be the stitchers of pamphlets, for they are ready sooner than bound books!

Blessed be he who lately wrote 'Cecil' (tho' it be but a novel), for it beguiled me thro' a weary night, & made me forget I had a pain in my side.

I cease the 'Kyrielle'★ of blessings for fear you should add 'blessed be he who first thought of <u>note-paper</u>, to confine women's correspondence within bounds'.

Yours truly, Dear Sir

Caroline Norton

★ Kyrielle: count all your blessings every day.

15

The Bible in Spain
George Borrow

———◆———

When the Norfolk traveller George Borrow arrived at Murray's in 1840 he had already used his remarkable linguistic skills to translate the Bible into several languages, including Basque, and had travelled widely in Russia and Spain. His first book, *The Zincali: Or an Account of the Gypsies of Spain* (1841), was followed by his very popular *The Bible in Spain* (1843) which he described to Murray as a queer book, because of its mix of genres and curious subject matter. Although quick of temper, and an intimidating figure at a burly six feet three inches, he established a respectful admiration for John Murray II. He was however disliked by the Murrays' friend Lady Eastlake who described him as 'a fine man but a disagreeable one'. John Murray IV and his brother Hallam were even more damning, calling him 'Scratch Man' as he had a habit of running after them as children and threatening to scratch their faces.

George Borrow to John Murray II, Oulton Hall, Lowestoft, Suffolk, 23 August 1841

My Dear Sir

It is quite possible that you will be glad to hear from me therefore I send you a line; I am tolerably well, and have no doubt that I should be better provided the weather were a little more genial, but it is truly melancholy – scarcely a gleam of sunshine: the farmers say that we shall have a wet harvest, which is a sorry proposal for me to whom the sun is necessary –

I live here quite retired and have not the least ideas as to what is going on save in my immediate neighbourhood. I still scribble occasionally for want of something better to do and hope by the middle of November to have completed my 'Bible in Spain'.

A queer book will be this same 'Bible in Spain', containing all my queer adventures in that queer country whilst engaged in distributing the Gospel, but neither learning, nor disquisition, fine writing, or poetry. A book with such a Bible and of this description can scarcely fail of success. It will make two nice foolscap octavo volumes of about 500 pages each. I have not heard from [Richard] Ford since I had last the pleasure of seeing you. Is his book out? I hope that he will not review the Zincali until the Bible is forthcoming, when he may, if he please, kill two birds with one stone.

I hear from Saint Petersburg that there is a notice of the Zincali in the Revue Britannique which has been translated into Russian. Do you know anything about it? With best and tender regards to Mr M. and family.

I remain
My Dear Sir
Ever most sincerely yours
George Borrow

Murray's at this time was a leading British publisher of Spanish works, including John Gibson Lockhart's *Ancient Spanish Ballads* (1841) and Lady Callcott's *History of Spain* (1840), Richard Ford's *An Historical Enquiry into the Unchangeable Character of a War in Spain* (1837) and *Handbook for Travellers in Spain* (1845). Ford had recommended Murray publish *The Zincali* and reviewed it positively. While Borrow was writing *The Bible in Spain* Ford wrote that 'I have given him much advice – to avoid Spanish historians and poetry like Prussic acid; to stick to himself, his biography, and queer adventures.' Murray sent Ford an early copy of *The Bible in Spain*, prompting this enthusiastic reply.

Richard Ford to John Murray II, Heavitree House, Exeter,
15 November 1842

My Dear Sir

Tomorrow I shall return to you the huge Labordes, with
many thanks & more apologies for having kept them so long
& what is worse unused; they have lain or 'lied' as the honest
vulgar would say on my table: they are truly French superfi-
cial & incorrect ad nauseam; one would think even a chien
de francais would never have gorged such stuff without
being sick, however we have our Murphy & perhaps he is
worse – arcades ambo & not worth the ink wasted in this
their condemnation.

I read Borrow with great delight all the way down per
rail & it shortened the rapid flight of that velocipede.

You may depend upon it that the book will <u>sell</u>, which,
after all, is the rub. It is the antipodes of Lord Carnarvon &
yet how they tally in whatever they have in common & that
is much; the people the scenery of Galicia & the suspicions
and absurdities of Spanish Jacks in officials who yield not in
insolence or ignorance to any liberal red tapists, hatched
in the hotbeds of jobbery and utilitarian mares nests. Dan
might take a hint as to the extracting of copper from rags &
Palmy for contempt of law national & international from
these local patriots' fire power – Borrow spares none of
them: I see he hits right and left & floors his man wherever
he meets him: I am pleased with his honest sincerity of
purpose & his graphic abrupt style; it is like an old Spanish
ballad, leaping in res medias, going from incident to incident,
bang-bang bang, hops steps & jumps, like a cracker, &
leaving off like one, when you wish he would give you
another touch or coup de grace: He is improved as a writer,

there are fewer sticking places, less poetry & quotation from
ponderous Spaniards. He has taken my advice in good part:
here & there he has got swampt in that damnable slough,
fine writing, but on the whole he has been true to himself
& his theme: he really sometimes puts me in mind of Gil
Blas – but he has not the sneer of the Frenchman, nor the
gilding the bad. He has a touch of <u>Bunyan</u> & like that
enthusiastic tinker, hammers away, a lo Gitano, whenever he
thinks he can whack the devil, or his man of all work on
earth, the Pope. Therein he resembles my friend & everybody's friend – Punch – who, amid all his adventures, never
spares the black one.

However I am not going to <u>review</u> him now: for know
that Mr L.[ockhart] has expressed a wish that I should do
it for the Q.R.; now a <u>wish</u> from my liege master is a
command. I had half engaged elsewhere, thinking that he did
not quite appreciate such a <u>trump</u> as I know Borrow to be.
He is as full of meat as an egg & a <u>fresh laid one</u>, not one
of your Inglis breed, long addled by over book making:
Borrow will lay you golden eggs & hatch them after the
ways of Aegypt; put salt on his tail & secure him in your
coop, and beware how any Poacher coaxes him with more
'raisins' or reasons out of the Albemarle preserves –

When you see Mr L. tell him that I will do the paper: I
had half enlisted elsewhere; but I owe my entire allegiance to
the Q.R. flag, & when 'called out' will ever fall into the
ranks; 'D—n Beaumonts Lead – & Blue & Buff birdlime'.
All my gitanesque learning & Borrow biography was put
into the paper which appeared on Mr Kemble's stage: now I
must do something quite light & lively – & your puff paste
is infinitely harder to make than dough, heavy & wet: I shall
send you back the <u>duplicate</u> sheets tomorrow; I have all

down to p.168. vol. III. Let me have the remainder ganando
horas [to save time] – i.e. per post & without delay: By the
way: you really should print at the end a glossary of the
words used in the text: Borrow a polyglott & talking to Jews
and Mesopotamians entre el duero [the Douro] – each in
their own lingo, forgets that country gentlemen at home do
not understand these strange lingoes: Of course he having all
these idioms at the tip of his tongue selects <u>exactly that one</u>
which best hits off, the <u>exact</u> intention in his mind; & all
languages have some of their own phrases which like
national dishes, are peculiar & have a flavour an ajo a
borracha [alcoholic garlic sauce] which is lost in translation:
perhaps my undertaking the <u>full force</u> of this 'gracia', makes
me <u>over partial</u> to this wild missionary: but I have ridden
over the same tracks, without the tracts, seen the same
people & know that <u>he</u> is true, & I believe that he believes
all that he <u>writes</u> to be true.

There are several errata & misprints which I intend to
send him: I write in great haste having a lot of accumulated
<u>local</u> bother. Perhaps if you see Mr L. you will tell him that
I will try my hand & if he does not like the result, there
need be no difficulty as the paper is 'booked' elsewhere: I
was delighted to see him in such force physical & spiritual.

Yours most truly
Rich. Ford

In the end Lockhart insisted on writing his own review for
the *Quarterly Review* (December 1842), with Ford's article
appearing in the *Edinburgh Review* (February 1843). These positive assessments promoted Borrow's international success, much
to his delight. In addition to many invitations to dine, he also
received, via Murray, an invitation to join the Royal Institution.

George Borrow to John Murray III, Lowestoft, Suffolk,
25 February 1843

My Dear Sir

I have received your letter of the 24th with the cards and letters: with respect to the Royal Institution, I hardly know what to say, had it been the Royal Academy I should have consented at once, and do hereby employ you to accept in my name any offer which may be made from that quarter; I should like very much to become an academician, the thing would just suit me more especially as 'they do not want <u>clever</u> men, but <u>safe</u> men'. Now, I am safe enough, ask the Bible Society, whose secrets I have kept so much to their satisfaction, that they have just accepted at my hands an English Gypsy Gospel <u>gratis</u>. What would the Institution expect me to write? (I have exhausted Spain and the Gypsies) though an essay on Welsh language and literature might suit, with an account of the Celtic tongue? Or would something about the ancient North and its literature be more acceptable? I have just received an invitation to join the Ethnological Society (who are they?) which I have declined. At present I am in great demand: a bishop has just requested me to visit him: the worst of these bishops is that they are skinflints, saving for their families; their cuisine is bad, and their port wine execrable, and as for their cigars – I say, do you remember those precious ones of the Sanctuary? A few days ago one of them turned up again, I found it in my great-coat pocket & thought of you.

I have read the article in the Edinburgh about the Bible – exceedingly brilliant and clever, but rather too epigrammatic, quotations scanty and not <u>correct</u>. Ford is certainly a most astonishing fellow; he quite flabbergasts me; handbooks, reviews, and I hear that he has just been writing a life of Velasquez for the penny cyclopaedia. Who wrote the article on 'Ministerial misrepresentations' could not be Macaulay: very poorly done, heavy to a degree, could not get through it.

It was the printer's fault and not mine that there has been delay, they had copy enough: all this week I have been expecting a proof in vain: I have written a second preface, very funny, but mild, I should wish you to see it before it is struck off. Do you think another edition of the Bible will be wanted soon & if so I must write another preface for that also. I have begun my Life: D.V. it shall beat anything I have yet done. Kind remembrances to Mrs Murray and the Ladies.

I remain
Dear Sir
Ever sincerely yours
George Borrow

P.S. Wife rather unwell.

Borrow did not join the Royal Institution or the Royal Academy. His later travels included a trip across Europe to Constantinople, but his further literary works were his partly fictional, partly autobiographical *Lavengro* (1851) and *The Romany Rye* (1857). His last major title was a travel book, *Wild Wales* (1862).

16

'Guide, philosopher and friend'
Murray's Handbooks for Travellers

———•———

During his travels on the Continent John Murray III noticed the lack of readily available and reliable information, so proposed to his father that they undertake a series of modern guidebooks. The resulting Murray's *Handbook for Travellers* series became the model for Victorian guidebooks, calling forth a host of imitators including the famous Baedeker guides, which followed the editorial style and content as well as the famous red bindings of Murray's. Murray's Handbooks, first published in 1836, enjoyed significant success and went on to cover all of Britain and Europe as well as Asia Minor, Egypt, India, Japan and New Zealand in over 400 titles and editions by the end of the century, when most of the series was sold off to travel specialist Edward Stanford as it had become too large and unprofitable for a general publisher. For some, though, the early progress in producing the British handbooks wasn't quick enough.

'John Bull' to John Murray III, London, 24 July 1846

Mr Murray

Why do you not publish a Handbook to England and Wales? I want one much – my Vary and my Paterson are ancient & worn out and my Capper is antiquated and bulky

– if you do not bring one out soon somebody else <u>will</u> – take my word for that.

I am

Your friend & patron

John Bull

P.S. My children go abroad too much – all your fault – if you would give them as good a Handbook to this country as they tell me you do to all outlandish places they would stay at home more. I repeat 'If you don't bring one out soon somebody else <u>will</u>.'

While Murray III undertook much of the writing and editing of the early volumes, including the first edition of the *Handbook for Travellers in Switzerland* (1838), they afterwards required numerous writers, editors and revisers, attempting to expand the national coverage as well as keep the details of transport, accommodation, routes and sights up to date. The deluge of correspondence this created included contributions from many famous people as well as the great mass of Handbook tourists keen to keep the guides accurate. Murray even provided a pre-printed form in each book to encourage additions and corrections.

The authority of Murray's Handbooks meant that inn owners and municipal authorities were wary of their power to promote or damn a place. George Stillman Hillard in *Six Months in Italy* (1855) wrote: 'From St Petersburg to Seville, from Ostend to Constantinople, there is not an innkeeper who does not turn pale at the name of Murray.'

In 1869 Murray was required to add a note that he had 'learned from various quarters that persons have been extorting money from innkeepers, tradespeople, artists, others, on the

Continent, under pretext of procuring favourable notices of them and their establishments in the Handbooks for Travellers'. As 'recommendations in the Handbooks are not to be obtained by such means' these impostors were to be dismissed as little better than swindlers.

German composer Felix Mendelssohn was keen to promote his friend and former guide's hotel. He wrote to his mother urging her to 'recommend the man and his house to all your correspondents. I am quite determined to write to London and ask Murray to praise the "Crown" in Meiringen, in his next red Guide-book to Switzerland; he can do so with a clear conscience. Michael has a good house, an extremely pretty wife, and five fine children.'

Felix Mendelssohn to John Murray III, Leipzig, Germany, 17 January 1843

Sir

I hope you will excuse the liberty I take, in writing these lines to you, if you still recollect that I had the honour of being introduced to you in former years, and I also hope that you will kindly grant me the pardon I am going to ask of you and by which you will confer a great obligation on me.

I travelled in Switzerland last year, while at Meyringen lived at Michael's Hotel de la Couronne. I knew Michael, who had been my guide on a former tour through that country, to be a good and honest and well educated man, and while I congratulated him to find him now in a good establishment, with a handsome wife and pretty children, he spoke to me of his further prospects in life of the wishes that were left to him, & amongst the last the most prominent was that, to be <u>named in your Guide</u> after the two other hotels. He told me he ~~had~~ did not know a way to attract your attention, as he was not able to write an English letter, & I instantly thought by myself that I would do it in his place. I lived there with a party of several ladies, and all agreed that the Couronne 'was as <u>clean</u> & <u>comfortable</u> an hotel as could be wished for', & they preferred the house with its Swiss architecture & the good and friendly manners of those within, to all the mock-grandeur which is now unfortunately so often found in Switzerland, and of which so many travellers have grown wearied. I can accordingly recommend my friend Michael with good confidence, & if ~~you~~ in the next edition of your Guide, you could insert the name of his hotel, you would render him most happy, & confer a true obligation on me.

It is not <u>before</u> but after the two hotels (of Wildenmann and the Reichenbach, both of which I also know & have been staying in) that it can be my wish to see it quoted, as it is smaller and newer than both; but in the qualities above mentioned it yields to none, and the view from its windows (which command the whole road up to the Reichenbach, and the Engelhörner with the adjacent glaciers) is more beautiful & extensive, than from either of them. I therefore believe and hope that it really deserves the honour which I so eagerly recommend it.

Excuse the liberty I have thus taken, & if you can grant my request let me know either by a line or by one of my friends there, that you will be kind enough to do so. I remain, sir

Your obedient servant

Felix Mendelssohn Bartholdy

Mendelssohn's advice was followed and the hotel was included in the next edition.

Lord Mahon, afterwards Earl Stanhope, to John Murray III, Lucerne, Switzerland, 6 September 1853

My Dear Sir

Pray thank Mr [Robert] Cooke for the extract from the Examiner which he had sent me. I have had a letter from Lord Brougham in reference either to that or to some other passage in the newspapers giving a quotation from my [History of England] fifth volume in its revised form, & I wish that you would be so good as to send His Lordship a copy of that volume to his house in Grafton Street.

We removed here yesterday from the Oberland district after a very prosperous ramble, deriving as usual the greatest advantage from your excellent Handbook. I assure you that all over this country it is honoured as it ought, & your verdict on inns serves as the chief motive of hope or fear with those who manage them. I am sure that if I boasted of your correspondence & confidence I might have been treated with princely honours & gone, if I pleased, scot free. So you see how powerful is the sceptre (or the Alpenstock perhaps!) which the editor of the Swiss Handbook wields!

Ever yours very faithfully
Mahon

Thomas Cook wrote and published travel guides and temperance literature, before developing tourist services in the 1840s. He went on to establish a world-famous travel agency undertaking British and foreign tours to countries such as America,

Switzerland, Egypt and Spain. The company took a keen interest in making sure Murray's Handbooks reflected its interests well.

Thomas Cook & Son to John Murray III, Ludgate Circus, London, 15 April 1880

Dear Sir

We are requested by the proprietor of the Hotel Rafaela at Burgos to call your attention to what we feel sure is an unintentional injustice to his hotel in your Handbook to Spain, where that hotel is described as being dirty.

From our personal experience and the experience of large numbers of our travellers we can safely say that the Hotel Rafaela leaves nothing to be desired in point of cleanliness.

We enclose you a letter we have received from Mr Oviedo for your perusal and shall be glad to receive your kind assurance that the paragraph will be withdrawn in future issues.

Yours truly
Thos. Cook & Son

Thomas Cook's son, John Mason Cook, invested heavily in Egypt, building a hotel in 1877 at Luxor and refurbishing the Nile steamers. The company was therefore concerned that Murray's *Handbook for Travellers in Egypt* should help promote Egypt and in particular John Cook's hotel, which was described as 'not good and the cuisine is poor and unsuited to invalids' and as for costs 'there are many extras which make it very dear'. Cook wrote to Murray to complain, receiving only a stock response. Years later he repeated his complaint to John Murray IV's brother Hallam.

John M. Cook to Alexander Henry Hallam Murray, Assouan,
Upper Egypt, 21 October 1887

Dear Sir

Your favour dated October 13th addressed to our chief office has been forwarded to me here for personal attention and from its contents I suppose you are not aware of the communications I addressed to John Murray Esq. some time during the summer of 1883 calling his special attention to the libellous statements appearing on page 450 of your Egyptian guide under the head of Luxor Hotels.

It happened very singularly that I had not seen the notice in question (although the edition is dated 1880) until my personal attention was called to it when I was in Egypt in the spring of 1883 & I naturally presumed that a communication from me to Mr Murray would have received at least an acknowledgement & an investigation but not having been favoured with any communication in reply I then gave instructions for Murray's Handbooks to Egypt not to be shown in the list of handbooks we recommended – I think you will see at once that I could not in justice to our business recommend a book which has a gross libel against ourselves.

At the same time I called attention to a very absurd notice on page 387 in connection with the steamers as follows: 'As the space in each steamer is limited it is better in order to make sure of a berth not to take a ticket until reaching Cairo.' To a certain extent the paragraph refutes itself because if the space is limited that is the very reason why passengers should book in London or other parts of Europe & so secure the limited accommodation & not wait until they get to Cairo & find it all taken.

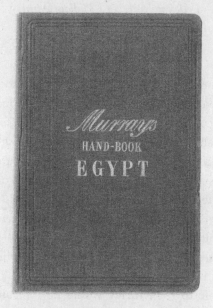

Your communication gives me the opportunity of putting the matter before you & at the same time assuring you that until my attention was called to the paragraph in question your books had always been placed prominently before the travellers & I have no doubt the accounts show that we have sold a considerable number of them.

I do not ask either you or any other publisher to say one word about Thos. Cook & Son's arrangements that you do not consider yourselves justified in saying as information for the travellers but I need scarcely say that when such a libellous statement is made as that re the Luxor Hotel I am perfectly justified in refusing to recommend the book containing it.

I am yours truly
John M. Cook
Managing partner of Thos. Cook & Son

The next edition of the *Handbook for Travellers in Egypt* (1888) noted: 'There is an excellent hotel belonging to Mr Pagnon, the energetic agent of Messrs Cook and Sons. It is well situated near the ruins of Luxor. Charge per diem (including everything but wine) 15s. . . . as the hotel is sometimes full, it is advisable to write or telegraph for rooms in advance.'

In addition to other British tourist guides, Murray's Handbooks' main rivals were the German-produced Baedeker guides which had originally been inspired by and directly copied from Murray's. Karl Baedeker's German language guide to Switzerland, first published in 1844, was one of their most popular and went through thirty-nine revised editions until 1937. A French edition, *La Suisse*, had twenty editions between 1852 and 1928. Baedeker also hoped to bring out an English edition, writing to Murray's after a rival guidebook appeared.

Karl Baedeker to John Murray III, Koblenz, Germany,
20 October 1852

[Translated from the French]

Dear Sir

During the course of the last summer, a certain Berlepsch, refugee and writer, well-known in Germany and Switzerland, and living in the latter country, published a guide to Switzerland which, based on the guide by my late father, was so successful that I shall have difficulty in making the point to him.

In Switzerland, where I spent several weeks this autumn with the sole aim of correcting this book, I learned that

Berlepsch is preparing an English translation of his guide. This publication may not do you any harm, sir, but if anyone should suffer, it will be me. The cause is a simple one. You must be aware, sir, that the number of tourists is increasing by the year. Not only rich people set out as soon as the weather improves, the lower classes vie with them in this respect. Students and others belonging to this latter class wish to know in advance more or less what their journey is going to cost them, what they will have to pay at hotels, tips etc. etc. It is the case that England provides its contingent of travellers just as much as do France and Germany, and I would venture to say that the small print run of the French edition of my late father's Swiss guide is taken up largely by the English. If, as a result, Berlepsch publishes an English version of his book, the English public will show its preference for him, naturally preferring this English edition to my French.

To avoid this drawback, I have to ask you, sir, if you believe that an English edition of Baedeker's Switzerland would be capable of doing you as much mischief, so that I may better judge, having regard to the amicable relationship which has always existed between you and my late father, whether or not to undertake such a publication. In my opinion, the public that purchases your 'Switzerland' and the one that equips itself with my father's simple guide, are two very different classes of buyer. The publication which I am planning would therefore be in no position to harm your book; should such an occasion arise, it would harm only Bradshaw and other publications of the same kind; as for me, I should be the only one to stand up against Berlepsch. I should not have dreamed of bringing out such a publication if I had not, as it were, been compelled to do so by the facts mentioned above.

Dare I ask you in conclusion, sir, to let me have your
reply as soon as possible. You will oblige me by doing so,
  Your very devoted servant
  Ch. Baedeker

Murray replied on 12 November 1862 that he was 'quite at a
loss to understand how an <u>English</u> Swiss Guide by Berlepsch
can injure you or even affect you at all. Your father published
his guide in German for Germans. It was founded and in part
translated from my Swiss Guide, which was written in English
for the English. Also your late father never lost sight of the fact
that my English Continental Guides gave him the idea, plans
and materials in the first instance for his German handbooks
. . . so strongly do I feel on the subject that if you persist in
the scheme, I shall publish a cheap Swiss Guide – French &
English – which I will take the utmost pains to circulate on
the Rhine and in Switzerland. If I write strongly, it is because
I feel strongly on this subject . . . I am utterly at a loss to
understand how you can suppose that such an English Guide
as you hint at could be circulated abroad without injury to me!'
  An English Baedeker only appeared after Karl's death in 1863,
published by his son, and saw twenty-eight editions until 1938.
  A generation later, Ernst Baedeker wrote to John Murray
IV to ask for his support in an exhibition he was curating on
the history of guidebooks.

Ernst Baedeker to John Murray IV, Leipzig, Germany,
26 November 1913

Dear Sir

You are no doubt aware that there is to be held next year
in Leipzig an <u>International Exhibition of the Book Industries</u>

and Graphic Art. A considerable part of the exhibition is to be devoted to an Historical Section illustrating the origin of writing and books and their development from antiquity to the present day. The various subsections are being dealt with by specialists in each department, and the undersigned has been entrusted with the commission to exhibit in a concise form, by means of a display of early volumes, pictorial illustration, etc., the History of the Guide Book.

It goes without saying that in any exhibition of this sort your handbooks ought to take a most prominent position. I am therefore applying to you for your kind assistance in this matter and for certain information which I require. I am indeed aware that Murray's Handbooks have been published for some years now by another firm; still I have no doubt that you are in the best position to answer the following questions.

1. When did the Murray's guidebooks appear, and which volume was it?
   [annotated: 1836 N. Germany]
2. Could I obtain a list of Murray's guidebooks, with information as to the dates the first editions appeared?
3. Does there exist a portrait (print or photograph), suitable for exhibition, of the founder?
4. I shall be very pleased and grateful if I might borrow some of the first editions for exhibition under glass. The books would, I need hardly assure you, be treated with the greatest care and would be returned to you unharmed at the close of the exhibition.

Any additional information, historical or statistical, concerning your Handbooks, would, of course, be extremely welcome to me.

Hoping to gain your interest and support in this matter.
I remain, Dear Sir
Yours very truly
Ernst Baedeker

Murray replied on 29 November 1913 with a list of Handbooks and their first appearance, and a generous offer of a collection of some of his father's original manuscripts for the exhibition 'on condition that great care should be taken of it, and that it should be insured against damage or loss, and that it should be returned in good condition'. Owing to the outbreak of the First World War these manuscripts and books were not returned until after the end of hostilities.

17

Typee
Herman Melville

———•———

The American Herman Melville's brother, Gansevoort, was responsible for interesting Murray's in his younger brother's account of his time on whaling boats in the South Seas of the Pacific Ocean in the early 1840s. His adventures, which included deserting his ship and living among the natives with his friend Toby, were published jointly in America as *Typee* (1846) and in Britain by Murray's as *A Narrative of a Four Months' Residence among the Natives of a Valley of the Marquesas Islands; Or, a Peep at Polynesian Life* (1846). Following the success of *Typee* came two sequels, *Omoo* (1847) and *Mardi* (1849). However Melville's writing generated widespread criticism concerning the authenticity and appropriateness of the story.

As a result of this and Murray's aversion to publishing fiction the company was not involved in Melville's most famous work, *Moby-Dick; Or, The Whale* (1851). During Melville's lifetime it sold far fewer copies than *Typee*, but after his death Melville's writings were held in increasing regard and critics eventually began to rediscover and appreciate *Moby-Dick*.

➢ ➢ ➣ ➢ ➣ ➢

Melville wrote to Murray to defend the truth of his work *Typee* and cited fellow castaway Richard Tobias 'Toby' Greene to support his case. His letters contained many variable spellings and errors, perhaps deliberately to reinforce the impression he wished to give of his poor education and seafaring background.

Herman Melville to John Murray III, New York, 15 July 1846

Mr John Murray

Dear Sir – The decease of my brother Mr Gansevoort Melville leaving me without any correspondant in London thro' whom to communicate with you, I waive cerimony & address you at once by letter. My object in so doing, is to inform you of certain matters connected with my 'Typee' which you ought to be acquainted with, & to allude briefly to one or two other subjects.

In the first place I have to inform you that 'Toby' who figures in my narrative has come to life – tho' I had long supposed him to be dead. I send you by this steamer several papers (N.Y. Courier & Enquirer, N.Y. Morning News, & Albany Argus) containing allusions to him. Toby's appearance has produced quite a lively sensation here and 'Truth is stranger than fiction' is in everybody's mouth. In Buffalo where he 'turned up' the public curiosity was so great that 'Toby' was induced to gratify it by publishing the draft of a letter which was originally sent to me. This is not the letter however, which appears in the papers I sent you. I was sorry for this on some accounts, but it could not be helped. However the impression which Toby's letter has produced is this – i.e. – that everything about it bears the impress of truth. Indeed, the whole Typee adventure is now regarded as a sort of romance of real life. You would be greatly diverted to read some of the comments of our western editors and log-cabin critics. But to the point. I am now preparing a short sequel to Typee containing a simple account of Toby's

escape from the valley as related to me by himself. This
sequel will be bound up with all subsequent editions of the
book here. The curiosity of all readers has been awakened as
to what became of him & now that he has appeared & his
story is so interesting, it naturally belongs to the narrative
that a sequel like this should be supplied. At any rate the
public are apprised of Toby's resurrection & are looking for
it. Besides, it is so strange, & withal so convincing a proof of
the truth of my narrative <u>as I sent it to London</u> that it
cannot be gainsaid.

Were it not for the long delay it would occasion, I should
take no steps towards the publication of any sequel until I
had sent the MSS to you. But as matters are, this cannot be
done – for there is a present demand for the book which
the publishers cannot supply – a new edition is in preparation – & after what has happened, this cannot come out
very well without the story of Toby. Still, if you publish the
sequel (which as a matter of course I suppose you will) no
one will interfere with the publication, since it will be quite
brief (perhaps not exceeding eight or ten pages) & depends
altogether upon the narrative which precedes it – Besides I
shall take care you receive a copy of it by the earliest
possible oportunity. Proceeding on this principle then, I have
rejected everything, in revising the book, which refers to the
missionaries. Such passages are altogether foreign to the
adventure & altho' they may possess a temporary interest
<u>now</u>, to some, yet so far as the wide & permanent popularity
of the work is conserned, their exclusion will certainly be
beneficial, for to that end, the less the book has to carry
along with it the better. Certain 'sea-freedoms' also have
been modified in the expression – but nothing has been
done to affect the general character & style of the book –

the narrative parts are untouched. In short – in revising the work I have merely removed passages which leave no gap, & the removal of which imparts a unity to the book which it wanted before. The reasons which will be given to the public for this step are set forth in the enclosed paper. Something like this will be published in the shape of a 'Preface to the Revised Edition'.

The new edition containing the Sequel of Toby will be out soon. This day the printers take it in hand, & will hurry it. A copy of it will be forwarded to you by the first steamer through the house of Wiley & Putnam. I would send you the MSS of the sequel, but it is by no means yet finished.

From the widely extended notices of 'Typee' which have appeared in England I am led to suppose that it has met with the most flattering success there. If this be so – it cannot be deemed premature in me to remind Mr Murray, of his having assured my deceased brother that in case the book met with 'unusual success' he would still further remunerate the author. Therefore, if you feel every way warranted in so doing (of which of course you are left sole judge) your early consideration of this subject will for special reasons be most gratifying to me.

As for the matter of the revised edition – if you publish one from the copy I shall send to you, I leave it to yourself to decide, whether I should be considered as entitled to anything on account of it. But however that part of the matter may appear to you – I earnestly trust that you will issue a revised edition. Depend upon it, sir, that it will be policy so to do. Nor have I decided upon this revision without much reflection and seeking the advice of persons every way qualified to give it, & who have done so in a spirit of candor.

I entertain no doubt but that the simple story of Toby will add very much to the interest of the book, especially if the public are informed of the peculiar circumstances connected with it. If you publish it, you will reap this benefit, whatever it may be in a pecuniary way; and altho' you will not be bound to pay me anything for the sequel, still, should you make use of it, I rely not a little upon your liberality.

I had almost forgotten one thing – the title of the book. From the first I have deeply regretted that it did not appear in England under the title I always intended for it – 'Typee'. It was published here under that title & it has made a decided hit. Nor was anything else to be expected – that is, if the <u>book</u> was going to succeed at all, for 'Typee' is a title <u>naturally suggested by the narrative itself</u>, and not farfetched as some strange titles are. Besides, its very strangeness & novelty, founded as it is upon the character of the book – are the very things to make 'Typee' a popular title. The work also should be known by the same name on both sides of the water. For these and other reasons I have thought that in all subsequent editions of the book you might entitle it 'Typee' – merely prefixing that single but eloquent word to the title as it now stands with you. If you try out the revised edition with the sequel – that would be the time to make this very slight but most important alteration. I trust that Mr Murray will at once consider the propriety of following this suggestion.

This is an unconscionable letter for a first one, but I must elongate it a little more.

I have another work now nearly completed which I am anxious to submit to you before presenting it to any other publishing house.

It embraces adventures in the South Seas (of a totally different character from 'Typee') and includes an eventful cruise in an English Colonial Whaleman (a Sydney Ship) and a comical residence on the island of Tahiti. The time is about four months, but I & my narrative are both on the move during that short period. This new book begins exactly where Typee leaves off – but has no further connection with my first work. Permit me here to assure Mr Murray that my new MSS will be in a rather better state for the press than the MSS handed to him by my brother. A little experience in this art of book-craft has done wonders.

Will you be so good as to give me your views about this proposed publication (it will be ready the latter part of the fall – <u>autumn</u> I believe it is with you) as early as possible.

Mr Murray must pardon the evident haste in which this long letter has been written – it was unavoidable. With much respect & esteem, Dear Sir, believe me

Very truly yours

Herman Melville

Despite Melville's insistence that his stories were true, doubts remained and he wrote again to urge his case on Murray.

Herman Melville to John Murray III, New York, 25 March 1848

My Dear Sir

Nothing but a sad failing of mine – procrastination – has prevented me from replying ere this to yours of the 17 January last, which I have just read over. Will you still continue, Mr Murray, to break seals from the Land of Shadows – persisting in carrying on this mysterious corres-pondence with an imposter shade, that under the fanciful

appellation of Herman Melville still practices upon your
honest credulity? Have a care, I pray, lest while thus parleying
with a ghost you fall upon some horrible evel, peradventure
sell your soul ere you are aware. But in tragic phrase 'no
more!' – only glancing at the closing sentence of your letter,
I read there your desire to test the corporeality of H—
M— by clapping eyes upon him in London. I beleive that a
letter I wrote you some time ago – I think my last but one
– gave you to understand, or implied, that the work I then
had in view was a bona-vide narrative of my adventures in
the Pacific, continued from 'Omoo'. My object in now
writing you – I should have done so ere this – is to inform
you of a change in my determinations. To be blunt: the work
I shall next publish will be in downright earnest a 'Romance
of Polynisian Adventure'. But why this? The truth is, sir, that
the reiterated imputation of being a romancer in disguise has
at last pricked me into a resolution to show those who may
take any interest in the matter, that a real romance of mine
is no Typee or Omoo, & is made of different stuff altogether.
This I confess has been the main inducement in altering my
plans – but others have operated. I have long thought that
Polynisia furnished a great deal of rich poetical material that
has never been employed hitherto in works of fancy; and
which to bring out suitably, required only that play of
freedom & invention accorded only to the romancer & poet.
However, I thought, that I would postpone trying my hand
at anything fanciful of this sort, till some future day: tho' at
times when in the mood I threw off occasional sketches
applicable to such a work. Well: proceeding in my narrative
of facts I began to feel an incurible distaste for the same; & a
longing to plume my pinions for a flight, & felt irked, cramped
& fettered by plodding along with dull commonplaces. So

suddenly abandoning the thing altogether, I went to work heart & soul at a romance which is now in fair progress, since I had worked at it under an earnest ardor. Shout not, nor exclaim 'Pshaw! Puhl!'. My romance, I assure you, is no dishwater nor its model borrowed from the Circulating Library. It is something new I assure you, & original if nothing more. But I can give you no adequate idea of it. You must see it for yourself. Only forbear to prejudge it. It opens like a true narrative – like Omoo for example, on shipboard – & the romance & poetry of the thing thence grow continually, till it becomes a story wild enough I assure you & with a meaning too.

As for the policy of putting forth an acknowledged romance upon the heel of two books of travel which in some quarters have been received with no small incredulity. That, sir, is a question for which I care little, really. My instinct is to out with the romance, & let me say that instincts are prophetic, & better than acquired wisdom – which alludes remotely to your experience in literature as an eminent publisher. Yet upon the whole if you consider the thing, I think you will unite with me in the opinion, that it is possible for me to write such a romance, that it shall afford the strongest presumptive evidence of the truth of Typee & Omoo by the sheer force of contrast – not that the romance is to sink in the comparison, but shall be better – I mean as a literary acheievement, & so essentially different from those two books.

But not to multiply words about it, I shall forward the proof sheets to you, & let you judge of it for yourself, for I have the utmost confidence in you. Supposing that you should decide to undertake the publication of this work; if you received the sheets by the middle of July next, could you have it out in thirty days from that time? And would you, under the circumstances, deem it advisable to publish at that season of the year, bearing in mind that there are reasons that operate with me to make as early a publication as possible, a thing of much pecuniary importance with me? If you say yea to these questions, then I think I should be ready to propose the following arrangement: that upon the receipt of the sheets & your decision to publish, you substitute £150 for the 100 guineas set down in your letter of December 3rd '47 – forwarding upon publication the former sum, & agreeing to pay me $1/2$ the profits of all future editions (should there be any) when all expences of outlay on your part shall have been defraied by the book itself; & remitting some specific memorandum to that effect, in case of accidents. If upon the receipt of the sheets you should agree to this, then without waiting to communicate with me, you might consider the matter closed at once & proceed to business at once; only apprising me immediately of the very earliest day upon which I could publish here. This would save time. In your next, will you point out the safest method of forwarding to you my book; seeing that Omoo met with such adventures at your atrocious Custom Houses.

By the way, you ask again for 'documentary evidence' of my having been in the South Seas, wherewithall to convince the unbelievers – Bless my soul, Sir, will you Britons not credit that an American can be a gentleman, & have read the Waverley Novels, tho every digit may have been in the tar-bucket? You make miracles of what are common-places to us. I will give no evidence. Truth is mighty & will prevail – & shall & must.

    In all sincerity yours
    Herman Melville

While Murray had given credibility and reasonable commercial success to some of Melville's works, they were largely forgotten during the author's last decades and he died in 1891 in relative obscurity, having suffered bouts of depression. Decades after his death his reputation underwent a revival and he is now considered one of the great figures of American literature.

18

Missionary Travels
David Livingstone

———•———

Scottish missionary David Livingstone became a national hero, in Britain and in many parts of Africa, as a result of his extensive explorations and ceaseless campaigning against slavery. His cause and reputation were greatly enhanced with his first book, *Missionary Travels and Researches in South Africa* (1857), which he hoped to have completed by Easter 1857, having agreed generous terms that January. However, it wasn't published until November as the process of writing, editing and illustrating the work was protracted, partly because author and publisher both recommended and consulted a wide range of experts and partly because Livingstone often resisted editorial interference with the text and was critical of the artists and engravers engaged in illustrating his book.

One such expert consultant was fellow African explorer Major Frank Vardon.

David Livingstone to John Murray III, Sloane Street, London,
28 April 1857

My Dear Mr Murray

You will oblige me if you let my African & English friend Major Vardon have a peep at the Falls. He is a good judge of lions and if you have the lion & myself by you I should like if you could shew him that too. I have got no slips lately.

I am &c

D. Livingstone

I would like him to see any of the animals you have by you as he is a good judge of what they ought to be.

The artist commissioned for the book was the appropriately named Joseph Wolf, much prized for the accuracy of his wild-life illustrations and their lifelike quality. However he wrote critically of his collaboration with Livingstone, recording: 'I used to go see [him] at Sloane Street; and he would propose subjects; but there was no <u>handle</u> to what he said. He had a thing in his mind that couldn't be illustrated. I couldn't make pictures of what he thought would be the best subjects. I didn't feel the inspiration to work with him.'

Wolf's depiction of the lion in Livingstone's famous near-death encounter solicited this distressed and annoyed outburst.

David Livingstone to John Murray III, Sloane Street, London, 22 May 1857

My Dear Mr Murray

Mr Clowes has just sent me proofs of the plates or draw-ings. The lion encounter is absolutely abominable. I entreat you by all that's good to suppress it. Everyone who knows what a lion is will die with laughing at it. It's the greatest bungle Wolf ever made. I told him about it and I told him the proportions were much too great on the side of the lion. It's like a dray horse over me. It really must hurt the book to make a lion look larger than a hippopotamus; I am quite distressed about it. Or at least make the lion smaller. Would the style in which Andersson's plates are got up not [be] superior to this? Of course I am no judge of this point but of the lion I am I think.

Is it impossible to put on a rag round the lions [loins] of these fellows? All wear something except the Batoka. I refer to the elephant hunt; to make the fellows all stark naked is worse than talking about urine and yet your critic turned up the white of his eyes at that.

The reception at Shinte's which came today is very poor. I have made some notes for the artist. My men ought to be close to me, two ficus or banian trees in the place and the roofs of the huts seen over the walls on one side as I have indicated. The musical instrument when seen sideways is thus. The keys are beaten with drumsticks. The drum slung on the neck & beaten with the hands.

Have you any of the permanent copy set up? I would like to see whether you [have faith] in the corrections introduced by your corrector, he is a man who has [no] sympathy in such a book. I don't send back the plates to Mr Clowes but to you, begging mercy against being caricatured.

D. Livingstone

Pray don't think me unreasonable; you may ask Vardon if you doubt.

Despite his keen interest in the artwork, Livingstone was even more insistent that his text, written in his own robust style, should not be interfered with.

David Livingstone to John Murray III, Hadley Green, Barnet,
30 May 1857

My Dear Mr Murray

I am sorry to find that you have been led to suppose that the reviser employed is in any way qualified for the work. I give you a few specimens of his erudition taken at random. Slip 98 line 22 from top, 'pestered' is the truth besieged is not; line 26th, spinal is not true it was uterine; but S 95, Hooping cough corrected into Whooping cough. What is that? 96, to his affrighted relatives corrected into to the great alarm of their astonished relatives!

No inspection of the body being ever allowed diluted thus, by these people! Then third line from top a line left out which is quite necessary to complete the sense. Please look at slip 111 and say whether what is struck out is not proof positive of your man being entirely wanting in sympathy with the author of a book of this kind. Prof. Owen puts stet opposite it.

S 210 bottom of page, does not know meaning of 'parts'! (vide Johnson or Webster) 213, makes nonsense of a plain statement in middle of page D[itto] D[itto]; 214, you see I have avoided saying expressly that the prepuce is cut off though it might be expected from using the proper term for that operation. And a man who puts his hand to revise a work on South Africa ought to have known the universal practice of the real cutting off yet see 218 – incision. See again 226, 'the phrase being identical with "abiit ad plures"' [gone to the majority, i.e. died] is struck out, by this gentleman – ab uno disce omnes [from one, learn all], ignorance I fear. Now, my good friend, I cannot think you have noticed the process of emasculation for which I fear you have been paying. The liberties he has taken are most unwarrantable and I cannot really undertake to father them. I am willing to submit my style, uncouth though it be, to Mr Elwin or any friend you like and if it is not clearer, more forcible and more popular than anything this man can give I shall then confess I am wrong. My letters written to the Geographical & Missionary societies are popular.

Why must you pay for diluting what I say with namby pambyism. Excuse me, but you must give this man leave to quit. I really cannot afford to appear as he would make me.

D. Livingstone

He reinforced these complaints the next day with the following letter.

David Livingstone to John Murray III, Hadley Green, Barnet, 31 May 1857

My Dear Mr Murray

I was extremely surprised and pained by the utterly unwarrantable liberties taken by the person you employed on my copy. I cannot believe that you are aware of them as you heard what Mr Elwin said about the pleasure he experienced in reading what I had written in my own style. I have the opinions of Prof. Owen, Sir Roderick Murchison, Mr Elwin & Mr Binney that it is more likely to be popular and saleable than if diluted or emasculated as this man has impudently presumed to do. It is therefore both for your advantage & mine that I reject in toto every change introduced in red ink. I am sorry you have been at the expense of employing this man. I will refund all you have expended on him if you please, but my dear friend every iota of his labour must go. I cannot and will not submit any one comma even to his judgment. The parts in which I have incorporated the corrections of Mr Binney can and must stand as I have put them. I have come to the conclusion since reading Kane's book today – set your man to that and I affirm he would erase & transpose more than in mine and yet that is popular. I think I may declare to you that you will not find me cantankerous or unreasonable or difficult to deal with in any other matter but I must positively resist any attempts to tamper with or emasculate the book. I am sure you have not looked at this impudent fellow's work seriously. It is quite abominable and no earthly consideration will make me succumb to make the work a mere primer. I fear, by the explanation I have given wherever obscure was marked it will even now partake of too much of the penny primer character. Many of the corrections already put in are not given in Kane's and my book will be read by persons in much the same position as to intelligence as the readers of his.

I send this before me but come up on Monday myself – I can get a man who has some sympathy with African travel, Galton for instance or Dr Archer. All the emendations I introduced in black ink must be retained. All those in red are nil. I would not for anything else give you one moment's pain but this is a case in which your interests will suffer as well as mine if allowed to go on. I cannot & will not submit to this unknown. I would do anything else for you but this you can't be aware of.

David Livingstone

As *Missionary Travels* was nearing publication Livingstone travelled around Britain and Ireland, being hailed as a national hero for his exploits.

David Livingstone to John Murray III, Liverpool, 13 October 1857

My Dear Mr Murray

I enclose the Preface and a rough copy of what I wrote when a little nettled at the pirates. The Preface on the white paper is for the printer, that on the blue is for yourself if you could suggest any point which might be transferred without making it appear coarse or vituperative. If not then throw it in the fire. Should you think proper to put in a softening expression anywhere pray do so though verily they don't deserve it. Edward Baines Esq of Leeds, the editor of the 'Leeds Mercury', wants an early copy for a friendly review in his paper and he will send the piece to you direct. I said I would give you his order. Mr Braithwaite of Kendal wants a number of copies and as he is a good friend of ours I shall feel obliged if you say to your man to pay particular attention to his orders. I would like to give a copy to Captain Need for his help with the pictures. I saw two photographs in Mr Mungo Murray's house, of the Zouga which in case of a second edition I could get. They shew the vegetation well. I meet the chamber of commerce here today & go to Birmingham tomorrow (14th); my address there is 'Spark Hill, Spark Brook, Birmingham'. I come to London on Saturday or Monday next.

D. Livingstone

The last sheet is between the printer, Admiral Smythe & Arrowsmith. The latter is the delinquent of course. Let him go on with the wood-cut. It is correct.

A substantial 20,000 copies of the first edition of *Missionary Travels* were printed and very quickly sold out.

19

'A most disagreeable office'
Literary Advisers

F aced with a deluge of manuscripts on a wide range of topics, each John Murray relied on a variety of increasingly professional readers to counsel him. Key among these were always the *Quarterly Review* editors, but Murray's also engaged paid literary readers and advisers, in particular drawn, for almost fifty years, from the Milton family, including from 1841 Henry (brother of Murray author Fanny Trollope) and from 1850 his son John. Both were civil servants in the War Office only considering manuscripts in their spare time. The latter, who advised on Livingstone's work, also appraised the manuscript of Algernon Swinburne's controversial *Poems and Ballads* (1866). After seven hours' reading he wrote a forceful and disapproving letter to Murray.

John Milton to John Murray III, War Office, Pall Mall, London, 28 February 1866

My Dear Sir

I cannot recommend you to publish these poems. I have read them as carefully as the author's very bad writing will permit. But I have failed to find a single line that has any poetry in it.

The author's published works are much better. They are formed on the classical model of the Greek Tragedies with whose spirit Mr Swinburne seems thoroughly imbued. But these lighter pieces are simply doggerel; there is no rhythmical flair in them – nor are there any poetical ideas. They never deviate into anything that can fairly be called poetry, so far as my poor judgement goes.

Yours very truly
Milton

Instead the poems were published by Edward Moxon. However, the day after the first reviews appeared in the *Athenaeum* and *Saturday Review* the book was withdrawn from sale on accusations of sensualism, immorality and blasphemy. Republished later in the year, by G. W. Carleton of New York, the volume continued to divide opinion, some hailing the new poetical style and explicit content of the verse.

Quarterly Review editor Whitwell Elwin's advice on literary manuscripts for Murray's tended to be direct and in some cases damning, as when he read Wilfrid Scawen Blunt's poetry. Blunt was equally known for his marriage to Lady Anne Blunt, Lord Byron's granddaughter and daughter of the computer programming pioneer Ada King, Countess of Lovelace. The Blunts travelled widely in the Middle East and preserved Arabian horse bloodlines at their stud breeding farm in Sussex.

Reverend Whitwell Elwin to John Murray III, Booton Rectory, Norwich, 23 April 1875

My Dear Murray

I fear that many persons write poetry because they are not able to write prose. They hope that the metre will conceal the poverty of the ideas. I am appalled to say that Mr Blunt is a versifier of this class. His pieces are really below criticism, and it would be wasting words to go into details. Moreover he appears to me to be an infidel, though it is difficult to be sure of the meaning he intends his lines to bear, writing as he does in such vague, misty language that you cannot tell what he is at. But the apparent drift of several of his pieces is rank infidelity, and perhaps atheism. I read some of the poems to my wife and when I commenced reading a sonnet beginning with the line, 'Why was I born in this degenerate age?' she said parenthetically, 'I should think because he was not fit for a better.' And certainly he has no right to complain of his lot. There ought to be no hesitation in peremptorily declining to countenance the poems in any way. Lord Lytton's opinion is nothing. He is warm-hearted; and friendly feelings with him always overpower his judgement.

I will write again, but keep Mr Blunt's poems today that I may save the post. I return the MS.

Always most sincerely yours W. Elwin

In the following scathing opinion of a drama by an unidentified judge, Elwin dissects its utter failure. It is as well that such scornful verdicts were not sent directly to authors, but rather to Murray himself who would mediate the rejection in more sympathetic and diplomatic terms.

Reverend Whitwell Elwin to John Murray III, Booton,
11 May 1865

My Dear Murray

There are four main ingredients in a drama – the plot, the characters, the incidents and the dialogue. The manuscript did not appear to me a success in any one of them. The plot excited no suspense, the characters were rather speaking abstractions than living realities, and the incidents were not sufficiently rapid and stirring. It is, however, on the dialogue that the author seems principally to have relied, and here also, I fear, he has failed. Unless blank verse is written with consummate skill it is only prose cut up into lengths, and the present drama is deficient both in metrical harmony, and variety of rhythm. The language, too, is without that peculiar felicity of expression which is essential to poetry, and I believe the writer would completely throw away his talents in cultivating a branch of literature which nearly everybody tries, and in which scarce anybody succeeds. The subject he has selected does not appeal to the sympathies of the present generation, but a better theme would do nothing towards remedying the other shortcomings.

I enjoyed my visit to London, & picked up a good deal of information. When Reynolds is done I may make another flying visit. I have not received the books which Cooke was to send after me. I am in no immediate want of them, & I only mention them in case they should have miscarried.

Lord Houghton is a good-natured man at heart, & will soon come round, unless the Archbishop has been giving himself airs, which is not improbable. I hope you will never hesitate to send me MS when you think my opinion will be of any use to you. It is no trouble for me to look them over.

Ever

Most sincerely yours

W. Elwin

All here are in perfect health, & desire kindest remembrances to you.

20

'The queen of science'
Mary Somerville

———•———

Despite being largely self-taught, Mary Somerville became the great populariser of nineteenth-century science, writing four books encompassing many subjects including astronomy, physics, mathematics, geography, geology, mineralogy, botany, optics and electromagnetism. To keep pace with the frequent advances in science her titles continued to be updated and remained popular with students and scientists throughout her long life.

Her first book was a condensed English translation of the Marquis de Laplace's five-volume *Mécanique céleste*, the leading work of astronomy of the day, which presented mathematically the nebular hypothesis of the solar system to explain its formation and evolution. *The Mechanism of the Heavens* (1831) was published at Murray's own risk, offering Somerville two-thirds of the profit and retention of the copyright. When the volume surprised them both by selling well, Murray refused even his small share of the profits, writing that he was 'overpaid by the honour of being the publisher of the work of such a remarkable person'. This cemented a long private and publishing relationship.

Even with Murray's generosity in publishing matters, as well as his assistance with substantial loans and helping her obtain a Civil List pension, Somerville and her husband often struggled financially. This, and her husband's poor health, persuaded them to move to Italy. However, their strong personal and business relationship continued to thrive through a regular correspondence.

Mary Somerville to John Murray III, Florence, Italy,
28 March 1857

Dear Mr Murray

I was much pleased to hear from Mr Pentland that the Council of Education has adopted my Phys. Geog. and that a new edition will be required immediately, but I must protest against going to press till it is brought up to the present time. Pentland wishes you to delay till June and so do I, for I am sure it is impossible to be ready sooner. I have already completely recast the chapter on the Ocean from Maury and shall have much more from that excellent work. I can have most of the journals from the Grand Duke's library, but I much want information on Africa, an article that must be entirely rewritten; perhaps you would have the goodness to send Livingstone's book and indeed anything that you think would be useful & sent by steam I shall have it in a fort-night. The gold mines in California and Australia were not discovered when the last edition was printed which will show you how far it is behind. You who are on the spot best know what is new, and can help me greatly – I shall work hard but I am not so ready a worker as I used to be, my hand shakes so much. I have excellent accounts of Mrs Murray and the children from medical friends and always hear of them and you with pleasure – we have all been well during the severe winter, unusually severe for Tuscany and even yet the weather is cold. Mr Somerville has never had a complaint till ten days ago when he caught cold and had a troublesome cough but I am happy to say it is nearly gone and he is well again.

I have just heard news that has surprised us not a little. Sir David Brewster, 76 years old, was married a few days ago to Miss Parnell, aged 26, a grocer's daughter. Sir David and his daughter have been living at Cannes which he left a few days before the wedding without saying a word to his daughter of his engagement but left her with the Duchess Dow. of Argyle who had to tell her of it. They were married at Nice and are going to Rome so we shall have a visit of the sposi on their way either going or coming.

I was delighted to hear that Woronzow's leg is quite well again but I fear he is too busy to take the exercise he requires. We all join in very kind remembrances to Mrs Murray and believe me

Ever sincerely yours
Mary Somerville

My Dear Murray – You will oblige me if you will procure & send me one of Mappin's Shilling Razor Strops – at No. 67 King William Street. Yours truly W. Somerville

Despite her avowed 'facility in mathematics', Mary Somerville got Brewster and his companion's ages wrong: he was seventy-five not seventy-six, she was thirty not twenty-six.

✦ ✦ ✦ ✦ ✦ ✦

Murray, keen to keep Somerville abreast of scientific and geographical developments, sent her recent publications, like those of Charles Darwin, including his *Descent of Man* (1871).

Mary Somerville to John Murray III, Naples, 5 April 1871

Dear Mr Murray

I thank you very sincerely for your valuable gift of Darwin which interests me exceedingly, although I believe that the prehistoric races of men were often little superior to mere animals, I cannot as yet pay due respect to the gorilla as my ancestor, but I am only reading the first volume.

I had a visit from almost all the astronomers who came to Sicily to observe the total eclipse, among others Mr Peirce who is professor of Math. & astron. in the Harvard University at Boston and superintendent of the coast survey of the US. Since he returned to America he has sent me one of the lithographic copies of a very remarkable work he has published on Linear Associative Algebra; it is difficult, and although I cannot study it for more than two hours at a time without being fatigued, I am happy to say I have not lost my facility in mathematics. I have several works bearing on the subject in question but I would be much obliged to you if you would send me Sir William Hamilton's Lectures on Quaternions.

Though I fear there will not be a second edition of my last work during my life, I have brought it up to the present year by adding Tyndalls on the colour of the sky, Huggins on the motions of the stars &c and lastly on the structure of the seas & the nature of the corona which according to the late observations will probably afford direct proof of the exertive of the chemical medium hitherto hypothesised though as if the undulatory theory of light and all its consequences depend. I am continually adding to the narrative of my Life so I have been very busy; besides during the war [of Italian unification] the newspapers occupied much of my time but I had plenty of it for the autumn and winter have been so bad that I could seldom drive out.

We had a very short visit from Pentland, he is so much disgusted with the state of Rome that I should not be surprised if he did not return; he will surely not pass through Paris in its distracted state. I have no sympathy for the French, they are so ungrateful for the bounty of England. The British fleet has been here for a short time. I had a visit from Admiral [unclear word] who is an old acquaintance; a first-rate ironclad remains supplied to be as a refuge for the Pope, but he seems to be inclined to remain at the Vatican protected by his troops.

Our beautiful view is shut out by a wooded building for a naval exposition and will be for some months which is great nuisance. I hear it does not promise much.

My daughters unite with me in kind remembrances to Mrs and Miss Murray –

Yours very sincerely

Mary Somerville

Old age did not dim her enthusiasm or ability for scientific and mathematical enquiry, and her fourth book, *On Molecular and Microscopic Science*, was published in 1869 when she was eighty-nine. Less than a year before her death, aged ninety-one, she wrote again to Murray that 'It is curious that I am as much at home on mathematical subjects as ever I was . . . I spend four or five hours every morning in studying theses.'

21

On the Origin of Species
Charles Darwin

———◆———

Charles Darwin's journal of his 1831–6 voyage on HMS *Beagle* was originally published in 1839 by Henry Colburn; however only a small number of copies was printed and Darwin received no form of remuneration. When he sought a wider readership, it was republished in a revised and more popular version by Murray's in 1845, on the recommendation of his friend, the geologist Sir Charles Lyell. So began a publishing and personal relationship that would last until Darwin's death in 1882.

Years after the reappearance of the journal, Darwin undertook to expand and publish his twenty-year-old notes on his theory of evolution, largely prompted by the intended publication of the strikingly similar theories of Alfred Russel Wallace. Concerned that Murray's might reject the work on religious grounds, he asked Lyell: 'Would you advise me to tell Murray that my book is not more unorthodox than the subject makes inevitable. That I do not discuss origin of man. That I do not bring in any discussions about Genesis &c, & only give facts, & such conclusions from them, as seem to me fair. Or had I better say nothing to Murray, & assume that he cannot object to this much unorthodoxy, which in fact is not more than any geological treatise, which runs slap counter to Genesis.' In requesting Murray to undertake the publication of his work,

Darwin's letter displayed an understandable mixture of anxiety and ambition.

Charles Darwin to John Murray III, Down, Bromley, Kent,
31 March 1859

My Dear Sir

I have heard with pleasure from Sir C. Lyell that you are inclined to publish my work on the Origin of Species; but that before deciding & offering any terms you require to see my MS. My work is divided into 12 chapters, as you will see in appended table at end of this letter. The Introduction, & 3 first chapters are <u>now</u> in 3 copyists' hands; & I hope to have them home in about 10 days. I defy anyone, not familiar with my handwriting & odd arrangements, to make out my MS till fairly copied. Ch. IV will be ready for copyist in 2 or 3 days. Ch. V–IX are all fully written out, but not finally corrected or copied; & would be very difficult to decipher. Ch. X is copied & is now in Dr Hooker's hands. Ch. XI is in copyist hands. Ch. XII, a short one, not even fully written out.

Now you will see state of work: I could send 3 first chapters well copied in about 10 days, & Ch. V–IX in the rough (but I must retain one Ch. not to be losing time) & Ch. X & XI well copied: but I would advise you to wait till more chapters are well copied. But, I will do, as far as I can, whatever you please; but the 3 first chapters & short Introduction cannot be sent till I get them back from copyists. At roughest calculation I think my MS will make about 500 pages of type & size of Lyell's Elements 1st edition.

It is the result of more than 20 years' work; but as here given, is only a popular abstract of a larger work on the same subject, without references to authorities & without long catalogues of facts on which my conclusions are based. The book <u>ought</u> to be popular with a large body of scientific & semi-scientific readers, as it bears on agriculture & history of our domestic productions & on whole field of Zoology, Botany & Geology. I have done my best, but whether it will succeed I cannot say – I have been quite surprised at finding how much interested strangers & acquaintances have become with the subject. Only some small portions are at all abstruse.

I hope to be ready for press early in May & shall then <u>most earnestly</u> wish to print at a <u>rapid</u> rate, for my health is much broken, & I want rest. I may add that I should have to beg for 100 or 120 copies at bookseller's price to give to many persons who have aided me.

Pray excuse the length of this letter. I shall be pleased if you approve of my work, & will undertake its publication.

Pray believe me

My Dear Sir

Yours very sincerely

C. Darwin

Introductory Remarks with <u>briefest</u> outline of whole book

I Variation under Domestication; or the origin & mode of formation of our domestic Productions

II Variation under Nature (short & dry chapter)

III Struggle for Existence (short & rather interesting ch.)

IV Natural Selection (important: parts rather abstruse)

V Laws of Variation (many curious facts)

VI Difficulties in Transitions of Organs & Beings

VII Instinct (interesting chapter)

VIII Hybridism (rather long & rather curious chapter)

IX Geological Succession of Beings on this Earth (long chapter)

X Geographical Distribution of Beings (long chapter)

XI Affinities; Classification: Embryology Rudimentary Organs (important & I think good ch.)

XII Recapitulation & Conclusion (short chapter)

Even without having the opportunity to read the full manuscript, Murray replied the next day: 'I hasten to thank you for your obliging letter of yesterday & for the interesting details regarding your work on Species contained in it. On the strength of this information & my knowledge of your former publications, I can have no hesitation in swerving from my usual routine and in stating at once, even without seeing the MS, that I shall be most happy to publish it on the same terms as Sir Charles Lyell's books.' That was a generous two-thirds of the profits to the author, which made Darwin nervous of the consequences when Murray did read it.

Charles Darwin to John Murray III, Down, Bromley, Kent, 2 April 1859

My Dear Sir

I am much obliged for your note, & accept with pleasure your offer. But I feel bound for your sake (& my own) to say in clearest terms, that if after looking over part of MS you do not think it likely to have a remunerative sale, I completely & explicitly free you from your offer. But you will see that it would be a stigma on my work for you to advertise it, & then not publish it. My volume cannot be mere light reading, & some parts must be dry & some rather abstruse; yet <u>as far I can judge perhaps very falsely,</u> it will be interesting to all (& they are many) who care for the curious problem of the origin of all animate forms.

I am glad to say that my copyists have been diligent & I find I shall be able to send you by post in 3 or 4 days, the Title (with some remarks for your consideration), the short Introduction, Ch. I & Ch. II (short but dryest in volume) & Ch. III. In about 8 or 9 days from now I shall be able to send Ch. IV & Ch. X & XI (& ultimately you can see all if you like) & these 6 chapters will give fair, but certainly not too favourable, notion of interest of whole work. Rely on it, that I shall work like a slave to complete all.

With my thanks & hearty wishes that you may not be disappointed in work, if published by you, pray believe me, My Dear Sir

Yours very sincerely

C. Darwin

P.S. I may as well mention that I shall require one diagram, engraved on copper on sheet to fold out; but it consists only of lines, & letters & figures, & cannot be at all expensive to engrave.

P.S. I would add that it is impossible for you or anyone to judge of real merit of my book, without reading the whole, as the whole is one long argument.

The diagram Darwin insisted on is perhaps the most famous in scientific publication: the tree of life illustrating the evolution of different species. Eventually the manuscript of *Origin* was submitted and Murray consulted his literary advisers for their opinion. Whitwell Elwin sent this lengthy letter, in which he expressed his deep misgivings about the work.

Reverend Whitwell Elwin to John Murray III, Booton Rectory, Norwich, 3 May 1859

My Dear Murray

I have been intending for some days to write to you upon the subject of Mr Darwin's work on the Origin of Species. After you had the kindness to allow me to read the MS I made a point of seeing Sir C. Lyell, who I understood had in some degree advised the publication. I had myself formed a strong opinion the other way & I stated to him fully my conviction & the grounds of it. When we had thoroughly talked the matter over Sir Charles considered that I ought through you to convey my impressions to Mr Darwin himself. I should have thought this presumptuous & impertinent in me if I had not received from Sir Charles the assurance that Mr Darwin would not consider it either the one or the other. Nevertheless I speak with diffidence, & am sorry that Sir Charles, who was just starting for the Continent, could not, before his return, find leisure to correspond with Mr Darwin on the question.

I must say at the outset that it is the very high opinion I have of Mr Darwin, founded on his Journal of a Naturalist, & the conviction, amounting to certainty, of the value of any researches of his which made me eager to get both him & his friends to reconsider the propriety of sending forth his treatise in its present form. It seemed to me that to put forth the theory without the evidence would do grievous injustice to his views & to his twenty years of observation & experiment. At every page I was tantalised by the absence of the proofs. All kinds of objections & possibilities rose up in my mind, & it was fretting to think that the author had a whole array of facts, & inferences from the facts, absolutely essential to the decision of the question, which were not before the reader. It is to ask the jury for a verdict without putting the witness into the box. One part of the public I suspect, under these circumstances, will reject the theory from recalling some obvious facts apparently at variance with it, & to which Mr Darwin may nevertheless have a complete answer, while another part of the public will feel how unsatisfactory it is to go into the theory when only a fragment of the subject is before them, & will postpone the consideration of it till they can study it with more advantage. The more original the view, the more elaborate the researches on which it rests, the more extensive the series of facts in natural history which bear upon it, the more it is prejudiced by a partial survey of the field which keeps out of sight the larger part of the materials. A second objection to the publication of the treatise in its present form, though of less weight than the first, is yet of some moment. The Journal of Mr Darwin is, as you have often heard me say, one of the most charming books in the language. No person could detail observations in natural history in a more attractive manner. The dissertation in species is, on the contrary, in a much harder & drier style. I impute this to the absence of the ~~facts~~ details. It is these which give relief & interest to the scientific outline – so that the very omission which takes from the philosophical value of the work destroys in a great degree its popular value also. Whatever class of the public he wishes to win he weakens the effect by an imperfect, comparatively meagre exposition of his theory.

I am aware that many facts are given in the work as it stands, but they are too often wanting to do more than qualify my criticisms. I state my views broadly & rightly. Mr Darwin will understand my meaning as well as if I had spoken with nice precision.

Upon the supposition that my description of the work is correct Sir C. Lyell agrees in my conclusions & bid me say this when I wrote you a letter for Mr Darwin to read. Sir Charles tells me that he feared that in his anxiety to make his work perfect Mr Darwin would postpone indefinitely the putting his material into shape, & that thus the world might at last be deprived of his labours. He also told me that another gentleman had put forward a similar theory, & that it was necessary that Mr D. should promulgate his conclusions before he was anticipated. Influenced by these considerations Sir Charles urged the publication of Mr D's observations upon pigeons, which he informs me are curious, ingenious & valuable in the highest degree, accompanied with a brief statement of his general principles. He might then remark that of these principles the phenomena respecting the pigeons were one illustration, & that a larger work would shortly appear in which the same conclusions would be demonstrated by examples drawn from the wide world of nature.

This appears to me to be an admirable suggestion. Even if the larger work were ready it would be the best mode of preparing the way for it. Everybody is interested in pigeons. The book would be received in every journal in the kingdom & would soon be on every table. The public at large can better understand a question when it is arrowed to a single case of this kind than when the whole varied kingdom of nature is brought under discussion at the outset. Interest in the larger work would be roused, & good-will would be conciliated to the subsequent development of the theory in all its bearings. It would be approached with impartiality − not to say favour & would appeal to the large public which had been interested by the previous book upon pigeons, which book would yet be complete in itself, & open to none of the objections that I have urged against the present outline. Indeed I should say of the latter that for an outline it is too much, & for a thorough discussion of the question it is not near enough.

I write this letter with the intention that you should forward it to Mr Darwin. He must be good enough to excuse the crude manner in which I state my impressions. I am obliged to write as fast as my pen can move or I should not be able to write at all. My sole object & desire is to secure his theory coming before the world in the way which will do justice to the extraordinary merit of his investigations & procure him that fame which belongs to him. I am but a smatterer in these subjects. What I say has no sort of authority except so far as it may chance to recommend itself to Mr Darwin's own reason. The book on pigeons would be at any rate a delightful commencement & I am certain its reception would be the best stimulus to the prosecution of his subsequent work. I should hope if he inclines to this view that the preparatory volume could soon be got ready for the press.

    Believe me
    Sincerely
    Whitwell Elwin

I have not quoted Mr Darwin's published work by its exact title. In fact, the title has been changed, & I never now know either perfectly.

Murray disregarded his trusted adviser's recommendations and coaxed Darwin through the often torturous publication process, with the first edition appearing for sale on 24 November 1859.

The annual meeting of the British Association for the Advancement of Science met in Oxford the following year. Although Darwin did not attend, his supporters, including Lyell, the botanist Joseph Dalton Hooker and leading zoologist Thomas Henry Huxley (nicknamed Darwin's bulldog for his ferocious defence of his friend), lined up against the Bishop of Oxford, Samuel Wilberforce, in one of the most famous scientific debates of the century. When the *Quarterly Review*, edited by Elwin, tackled *Origin* it was to Wilberforce, not a Darwin supporter, that Murray turned. Wilberforce criticised Darwin's evolutionary theory, arguing it was 'a dishonouring view of Nature' which was 'absolutely incompatible' not only with the word of God but the 'moral and spiritual condition of man'. Murray sent a copy of the review to Darwin.

Charles Darwin to John Murray III, Down, Bromley, Kent, 3 August 1860

My Dear Sir

I suppose that I have to thank you for a copy of the Quarterly, which I found here on my return home. The article on the Origin seems to me very clever & I am quizzed splendidly; I really believe that I enjoyed it as much as if I had not been the unfortunate butt. There is hardly any malice in it, which is wonderful considering the source whence many of the suggestions came. The Bishop makes me say several things which I do not say, but these very clever men think they can write a review with a very slight knowledge of the book reviewed or subject in question.

With my thanks for your kind present

Pray believe me

Yours very sincerely

C. Darwin

I see there is a cancelled page, which I presume contained some great blunder; what sweet revenge it would have been, had but the page been left in! Did you ever read such magnificent nonsense as the 'strong shudder which ran through all this the world'!

The passage that Darwin quotes reads fully and correctly: 'But we can give him a simpler solution still for the presence of these strange forms of imperfection and suffering amongst the works of God. We can tell him of the strong shudder which ran through all this world when its head and ruler fell.'

His tempered response to such a savage review was not matched by his supporters, with Hooker sending this outraged letter.

Joseph Hooker to John Murray III, Kew Gardens, London, 1860

<u>Private</u>

My Dear Murray

Pages 251, 252 have been <u>cut out</u> of my copy of the Q. Review & of all others I have seen! Also my copy wants a slip of <u>6 Errata</u> in the Darwin article, which I find in the copy at the Athenaeum.

The article itself is astonishing & one does not know what to wonder at most − its eloquence, ability, utter mis-apprehensions of the facts of Darwin's book, appalling ignorance of the rudiments of science, or incredible blunders. Owen has made a tool of the Bishop, who has unwittingly fallen into all his (Owen's) snares, & exposed himself to the ridicule of all naturalists. Scientific men have a right to be protected against a leading journal entrusting a scientific book to an intemperate reviewer, & the Review must assuredly wish [to] be protected against [word unclear]. I am extremely sorry for it, though it will do Darwin's book all the good in the world.

I am ever yours
Jos D. Hooker

Darwin was generally forgiving of his opponents and critics. He modestly wrote: 'I have almost always been treated honestly by my reviewers, passing over those without scientific knowledge as not worthy of notice. My views have often been grossly misrepresented, bitterly opposed and ridiculed, but this has been generally done, as I believe, in good faith . . . On the whole I do not doubt that my works have been over and over again greatly overpraised.'

Origin went through six editions during Darwin's lifetime. Murray's and Darwin together produced eleven titles in more than 150 different authorised editions, with over 94,000 copies sold. Darwin reckoned that he had made £10,248 from his books.

22

'He thinks he knows as much about printing as he does about digging'
Heinrich Schliemann

Having made his fortune, German businessman Dr Heinrich Schliemann dedicated his life to proving the historical reality of the Homeric Trojan Wars. After his discovery in 1873 of a treasure hoard at Troy, in present-day Turkey, he excavated the Greek sites of Mycenae and Tiryns and discovered further treasures, which he wrongly but convincingly associated with the era of the Trojan Wars. His books were extravagantly illustrated with hundreds of photos taken on site, and their production was made possible by his willingness to subsidise the high costs entailed. Murray's lavish editions of *Mycenae and Tiryns* (1878) and *Troya* (1884) had gold-embossed bindings designed by Hallam Murray.

John Murray III had first approached Schliemann to translate some of his works on Troy for the *Quarterly Review*.

Dr Heinrich Schliemann to John Murray III, Athens, Greece, 5 April 1874

Dear Sir

In answer to your esteemed favour of 26th ult. I beg to say that I have nothing against it if you translate and publish in England my 'Trojanische Alterthümer' along with a selection of copies of the photographic illustrations accompanying that

work, provided you pay for my account fifty guineas at the
bank of Messrs John Henry Schroder & Co in London and
you give me twenty copies of your publication of the work.

I would advise you by all means to get the work translated
from the German and not from the French edition and to call
attention of your translator to the word 'Keil' instead of which
he must read 'Beil' (hatchet) as explained in the preface.

I have all your publications and I hardly need tell you
that I have read them with admiration.

I am

Dear Sir

Yours faithfully

H. Schliemann

Following Murray's publication of the translated work, he
published the extensively illustrated *Troy and its Remains* (1875).
Meanwhile Schliemann's removal of the Trojan treasures from
Turkey became mired in controversy and legal suits.

*Dr Heinrich Schliemann to John Murray III, Athens, Greece,
3 December 1874*

My Dear Sir

I was happy indeed to see in the Times that you sold
to the London booksellers above 800 copies of the 'Trojan
Antiquities' and congratulate you most heartily with this
splendid success. I strongly advise you to print at once 5,000
copies for your first edition, for this number you can, I
believe, easily sell in the United States alone by the ingenious advertisements by the all-powerful press. Mind that your
work can never lose its value and that it will be enquired for
for ages to come.

When you have done with the drawings of the whorls, made by the director of the French school Mr E. Burnouf and his talented daughter, please return to me <u>at once</u>, for they belong to these friends who merely lent them to me for your work. When you have done with the other drawings and photographs please preserve them carefully until I come myself.

I am happy to add that in all probability my Turkish lawsuit will be terminated in the course of a fortnight by a payment in cash and an engagement to continue the excavations in Troy for 3 or 4 months for the benefit of the Imperial Museum. Of course I do <u>not</u> give up anything of my collection.

I am

My Dear Sir

Yours very faithfully

H. Schliemann

Schliemann, writing from Athens on 4 March 1875, acknowledged Murray's role in producing a stunningly beautiful book: 'Only great things I expected from Mr John Murray, but in the present instance this celebrated publisher has surpassed himself and the volumes before me <u>far exceed</u> my most sanguine expectations. In fact they are an object of wonder and astonishment to me and to all my friends here and beyond all praise is the care you have bestowed on it. Not only the editor, Mr Philip Smith, is a <u>great scholar</u>, but the engravers, the printer and even the bookbinder have done wonders under your <u>genial</u> direction. Please accept, together with my thanks, my hearty congratulations with this amazing success; may this magnificent publication repay your trouble thousandfold!'

However, Schliemann could be equally unappreciative and critical. When his *Mycenæ* (1878) was being prepared he wrote to John Murray III, on 25 February 1877: 'this is an extraordinary work on the most extraordinary and grandest discovery of all ages, on a discovery which can <u>never</u> be excelled by man, and therefore it is necessary that it should be done with the greatest care and attention . . . Without me the thing will be a chaos to any editor and the book can never be edited without hundreds of mistakes.' Murray was further induced to use his friendship with William Gladstone to persuade the latter to write a preface, thereby adding legitimacy to Schliemann's work.

John Murray III wrote to his son John Murray IV in 1876: 'Schliemann thinks he knows as much about printing as he does about digging – which he doesn't. Witness his absurd idea of printing off his book in a week. I expect he will come over and you will show your tact in soothing & managing him.'

Their relationship did not improve when Schliemann wrote to Murray: 'I am not anymore your friend because you degrade me before Mr Brockhaus [the German publisher] and you degrade me before the English people.' Murray, the seasoned publisher, took all this in his stride and all ended calmly with Murray writing, '[I] am proud to be associated with you.' Murray's reputation remained intact even when Schliemann became a figure of great controversy for his questionable archaeological practices, which included rearranging finds, incorrectly attributing them to more heroic periods and even commissioning fake items for him to discover!

23

Self-Help
Samuel Smiles

———————◆———————

Scottish doctor and railway company secretary Samuel Smiles began lecturing to working men's clubs and societies in his spare time, to inspire the men with examples of hard work so as to better themselves. Following his surprisingly successful biography of railway engineer George Stephenson, he was encouraged to collect his biographical fragments together in a volume called *Self-Help; with illustrations of character and conduct* (1859), which was a precursor to the modern genre. This collection of biographical sketches and inspirational anecdotes of self-made men not only caught on in Britain, where it sold over a quarter of a million copies in the nineteenth century alone, but was also translated into over forty foreign languages.

Murray's was naturally keen to encourage Smiles to write works in a similar vein, which he did with *Character* (1871), *Thrift* (1875), *Duty* (1880) and *Life and Labour* (1887). Smiles's books were a phenomenal international success, being translated into dozens of languages. In Italy his books went through even more editions than in England, which encouraged him to visit the country.

Samuel Smiles to John Murray IV, Hotel Quirinal, Rome, Italy,
30 March 1879

My Dear Sir

Will you kindly direct a copy each of 'The Scotch Naturalist' and 'Robert Dick' to be sent by post to Prof. Scultor Rossetti, Via Marguta, Rome.

I brought these books with me intending to present them to the sculptor – who, as you know, has executed a very fine statue of 'Self-Help' – a girl plaiting her hair, and with the book upon her knee, reading it while she is doing her dressing, & thus making the most of her time – but I have given one of them to Signora Cairoli, wife of the late Prime Minister, who translated 'Character' into Italian; and I have asked her to present the other to the Queen of Italy. I was introduced yesterday to Cairoli & his lady. You may remember that Cairoli in a measure saved the King's life when riding through Naples a short time ago. He received me with great politeness, & gave me a hearty pump of his hand. It is a misfortune for me not to speak Italian, but the synora speaks English very well, and was able to interpret my conversations. It was then that she told me that she had translated 'Character', which, she said, had given her so much pleasure. She was pleased to say that I was the only living writer who devoted his time to elevating the people by pressing upon their consideration moral & social subjects, and that my books had been about the best read and were the most valued in Italy. Of course, this was a great gratification to me and endorsed that article in the Quarterly, for which I cannot thank you & the author too much.

I was a fortnight in Rome on my way south to Naples. I

did not deliver my letters until my return; and now I am almost overwhelmed with invitations. While at Naples, I saw Pompeii, went on to Sorrento, Capri, etc.; went round the Bay of Baiae, and greatly enjoyed the scenery & the ruins of Roman greatness. I returned near a week ago, and intend to stay another fortnight.

I staid a week at the Europa, but found the accommodation bad, and the dinners half cold, and dear. I removed here & found everything most comfortable. At Naples I staid at the Royal Hotel des Estrangers. It is entirely new, & a very fine hotel, close to the Washington. It has been removed from the place in the Guidebook, and that paragraph will have to be altered.

> With regards to Mr Cooke, John the third, and all at 50 A. St
> Believe me ever
> Yours very faithfully
> S. Smiles

Not all, however, were equally enamoured of Smiles's book.

Philip Kent to John Murray IV, London, 27 April 1892

Gentlemen

I am penning a scathing criticism of Smiles's <u>Self-Help</u>, which is — as the title of my article describes it — a 'Century of Errors', which stamp the author of <u>Self-Help</u> as a pretentious dunce.

I doubt whether his title of LLD — <u>bought</u> doubtless from a Scotch university — will avail to shield him from an attack giving chapter and verse, and written by a man who did not buy his degrees, but received them — whatever their value — from Cambridge and the Inner Temple.

But 'tis open to you, the publishers of this much puffed piece of shoddy, to buy my article, if you please; on condition that my corrections shall be embodied in the next edition. Thus both my objects in writing the article will be gained. But 'tis for you to decide, gentlemen, whether you deem it worth while to make peace with the enemy of your 'wares' while you are in the way with him.

Your obedient servant
Philip Kent

Kent's letter was unsurprisingly not actioned or answered. Others were inspired by Smiles's message of self-improvement. Almost a century after its first publication the literary critic Rebecca West wrote to John Murray VI: 'Thank you so much for sending me SELF-HELP. My mother and I had an interesting revelation of its widespread effects when she took me abroad for my first trip and we stayed in southern Spain, where we met a man who said he had only been able to build up a large business as a smuggler owing to the inspiration given him by Mr Smiles. I feel this cannot have been Mr Smiles' intention.' Another, more appropriate, recipient of Smiles's message was this aspiring young writer.

Renee Hopkins to John Murray IV, Kidderminster, 27 March 1921

Dear Sir

I have just been reading one of the books that you have published and I must say it has fired me with great ambitions. It is Samuel Smiles' 'Self-Help' which, as you know, tells of men who have risen from humble origin to great fame, just through sheer perseverance.

I had never heard of this book until it was presented to me as a prize for good composition and the one who distributed the prizes said that he hoped we should one day be a credit to our school and our town, and I think that from that time I have done nothing but dream of the day when I could do something for myself.

I know it is quite impossible for me to be a second Mrs Gaskell, Louisa M. Alcott, or Harriet Beecher Stowe, but still I want to try to do something.

Since I started school (I am fourteen now) I have generally been at the top of composition, not the story part so much as in descriptive essays, at which my headmistress said I was excellent. Please don't think I am praising myself, but I am doing this entirely on my own with nothing to help me except my own common sense, imagination & nature's works to give me ideas.

I am telling no one of my secret ambition so that no one can laugh at me if I fail. I have been working in an office since I left school at Christmas but was forced to give it up because of my health so you see I must do something or I shall be a great disappointment to Mother and Gran.

I know very little about the publishing of books, and I want to know if you charge very much for publishing. I hope it is not very much for we are very poor and cannot afford large sums of money.

So would you explain everything to me please for I am anxious to see how my little essays turn out.

You will find enclosed an essay on a 'Gipsy Encampment' that I wrote when I was nearly thirteen. Do you think I could improve upon this style or is it too slow for the hurry & scurry of modern life? If I should succeed I want, when I am older, to write a story based on my own life with many fictitious incidents and a few real ones for my life has been anything but uneventful.

I enclose a stamped envelope for your answer and if I succeed you can have some more essays & choose the best from them as you wish.

I remain

Yours faithfully

Renee Hopkins

I have written a great many more essays that I think are much better than the one enclosed; would you like to see them before you tell me that they will be of no good to you?

Murray sent a prompt reply: 'I am always interested to hear of any young people who aspire to become authors, but I have to warn them (and you among them) that it is no easy task, and requires much study; and, often failure and disappointments must be expected.' He then went on to criticise her writing and recommend reading good fiction such as Sir Walter Scott, Jane Austen and Robert Louis Stevenson. He also recommended she read one of his own books, Cope Cornford's *Essay Writing for Schools* (1903). His final postscript advice was 'Don't think of paying a publisher to bring out a book. If a book is worth publishing a good publisher should pay for the production.'

24

'I will say all the good of Pope I can'
The Works of Alexander Pope

———◆———

In addition to his role as editor of the *Quarterly Review* and advising on manuscripts, Murray's engaged Whitwell Elwin to produce a major new edition of the poetry, letters and life of the early eighteenth-century poet Alexander Pope, of whom Elwin had a mixed opinion, being less fulsome in his admiration than many contemporaries. Pope's reputation was based on his satirical verse, heroic couplets and his translation of the poetry of Homer, all making him frequently quoted and much admired throughout the nineteenth century. Elwin initially produced two volumes of poetry and three of letters (1871–2), but he later became dissatisfied with the work.

Reverend Whitwell Elwin to John Murray III, Booton Rectory, Norwich, 6 January 1871

My Dear Murray

I shall be delighted to read the poetry, which has not, however, arrived, nor the vol. of Pope which Cooke announces. They will probably come tomorrow.

I rejoice to receive your suggestions, & will say all the good of Pope I can, though I expected, & still expect to be much attacked for speaking no better of him. This will do the edition no harm, for the public have no objection to criticism on Pope or on anybody else, even when they blame it. Far from having any spite against the poor little man I am only sorry I am obliged to be so hard upon him. As to his poetry I praise it quite as highly, & censure it less bitterly, than any great critic who has already examined it in recent days – De Quincey, for instance, who was a consummate judge. My language is tame to his. The thrust is that very much of Pope's verse is commonplace, & his genius is confined to the Rape of the Lock, the Epistle of Eloisa to Abelard, the Dunciad, & particular passages of the Satires. This will be universally recognised in a few years. In the meanwhile my opinions seem more peculiar than they really are because the newspaper critics are not well read in the profound criticism of Coleridge, De Quincey etc. But still I am obliged for your hint, & will do my best to show the sunny side of the peach.

Always
Most sincerely yours
W. Elwin

I am delighted that dear old Panizzi approves. I have a very good friendship for him.

In the following letter, before discussing Pope again, he disparages an unknown poet whose work he despises.

Reverend Whitwell Elwin to John Murray III, Booton Rectory, Norwich, 7 January 1871

My Dear Murray

Of all the verse I ever read this, I think, has the least pretension to the name of poetry. The thoughts are obscure, the sentences are intricate, the metre is halting & unmusical, the language is overstrained, & yet without force, the general vein of sentiment is dull & lifeless, & in addition, the Soliloquy of Pontius Pilate is shocking to reverence. From beginning to end there is not one happy line. The writer is under a huge delusion. If he is a man of name his verse will mar his reputation, & if he is obscure the poems will die in their birth. Nothing except a name could sell them, nor would any name float them for more than two or three months. In your place I would at least advise him to suspend their publication till his MP life has terminated, or he will damage his position in the House of Commons, & perhaps lose his seat at the next election. He should read Shakespeare's Julius Cesar, & take warning by Cinna, who was torn to pieces by the mob for his bad verses. I have really nothing more to say of them, for they are utterly worthless, without any one element of beauty or power, & it would not alter my opinion if it turned out that they were produced by the united wisdom of the cabinet. They seem, however, more like the effusions of a wandering mind, & are, perhaps, the work of poor John Bright in his illness.

Archbishop Whately said that when a book met with general approval that it was proof that it was not much wanted. Because people approve their own opinions, & their praise was evidence that the ideas were stale. There is a good deal of truth in this, & it will take some time to reconcile many people to a view of Pope which runs counter to their prejudice. If they are unable to answer the evidence they will not the least rebel against it, & on these occasions they follow the Old Bailey precept, 'No case; abuse the prosecutor.' But truth prevails in the end, & it is to this that we must look. Still, I know that I, too, must err sometimes, & I am glad to weigh points very carefully where I may be supposed to be wrong. Yet even with respect to the poetry, it is not possible to avoid opposition to the traditional, nothing for the general public have not hitherto drawn the line between Pope's good poetry & his bad, though it has been drawn pretty clearly by enlightened critics. On one point the common delusion is curious – Pope is believed to be the most correct of poets, and he is indubitably the most ungrammatical of any eminent poet in the language as was long ago remarked by both Hazlitt & De Quincey.

Always

Most sincerely yours

W. Elwin

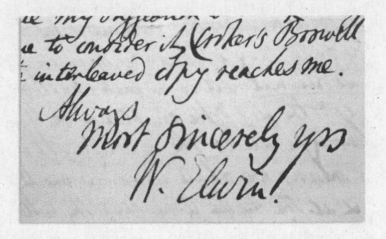

After Elwin had received Murray's generous donation to the building works at his church, he wrote to express his thanks and to suggest that someone take over his editorial duties on Pope. He was also engaged by Murray to consider the viability of a new edition of James Boswell's works, building on the success of John Wilson Croker's popular ten-volume edition of

Boswell's *Life of Samuel Johnson* and other works (1831–9); however no new edition was forthcoming.

Reverend Whitwell Elwin to John Murray III, Booton Rectory, Norwich, 13 June 1878

My Dear Murray

You & Cooke are most generous always, & it is very munificent of you to send me this cheque. You will have to add another obligation, which is to come & see the chancel when it is finished for it will really be lovely, & have a distinctive character of its own as all buildings ought to have. If all goes well it will be finished I think about the end of the year & it will be a double pleasure that you & Cooke should see the chancel & that we should see you in Booton. In the meanwhile there is still a great & separate pleasure to us in your splendid benefaction. So a thousand thanks to both of you.

The best editor for Pope would be some rather young person imbued with literary tastes, who being enthusiastic in his work will not grudge the pains which the undertaking requires. Nearly all men in London get soon into hack ways of doing literary work & will not put over-much labour, research, & thought into it. But a man fresh to the pursuit loves it for its own sake, & will give himself to it heart & soul. I would do my very best to help him. You might at least look round & see if there is not some clever, hopeful person of the kind that would be glad of such an opening for his tastes & talents.

I will do the Boswell gratefully to the best of my ability. I will work at it till the end of the year in all my leisure time, & will then send you the result to look over. You shall

then decide whether you will like to go forward in it &
until then I would not have you alter your advertisement. I
consider that 4 volumes will be ample — three for the Life &
Four to the Hebrides, & one for the Johnsoniana. I will use
whatever Croker is useable, & will treat him with respect or
silence. The crying vice of this mind was that he constantly
preferred something of truth. No more today except that I
am always

Most sincerely yours
W. Elwin

On receipt of this letter, Murray lost no time in offering the
editing of Pope to William John Courthope, a young literary
man in the mould that Elwin had recommended. During the
course of the 1880s Courthope completed the ten-volume life,
letters and poetry edition of Pope, which was widely praised
as a model of such works.

25

'A heaven-sent faculty for having adventures'
Isabella Bird

Despite frequent ill health and the prevalent misogyny of her day, Isabella Bishop, née Bird, was one of the most remarkable travellers of the nineteenth century whose wide-ranging journeys frequently involved danger and hardship. Her first book with Murray's, *The Englishwoman in America* (1856), had been a relatively tame affair, relating her travels around east coast churches. However, her more adventurous travels in middle and old age captured the reading public's attention. Later in life she embraced peril; she rode thousands of miles: on elephants in the jungles of Malaysia and, at the age of seventy, on horseback with the Berbers over the High Atlas Mountains. She completed an 8,000-mile round trip of the Yangtze valley, climbed an active volcano in Hawaii and scaled 14,000-foot mountains in Colorado. This last trip provided the source material for *A Lady's Life in the Rocky Mountains* (1879) which was generally very well received, including by *The Spectator*.

Isabella Bird, later Bishop, to John Murray III, 16 Oakley Square, London, 11 November 1879

Dear Mr Murray

The reviewer in the Spectator must have been inebriated when he wrote the review of my book. I shall be ashamed of meeting anyone who by any chance can have read it. I suppose I ought to be very much pleased. Other notices if any are given will doubtless cut it up in an equally exaggerated fashion, your flattering judgement of it being the mean between the two.

I hope it may help to float my Japan book.

I sent the MS back in good order, with the illustrations arranged, but there must be some others, such as myself in a rain cloak which belong to the same letters. I think the bundle sent nearer 3/4 than 2/3.

Kindly let me know the selling price and the trade price of the Rocky Mountains?

Lady Parks is I fear actually sinking. All we can hope for now is that she may live until Sir Harry arrives, which cannot be before Monday.

I am not near so well which is disheartening.

Yours sincerely

Isabella Bird

Not all reviewers were as complimentary as *The Spectator* had been. A critic in *The Times* of 22 November 1875 commented on her riding clothes while in the Rocky Mountains, suggesting that her Hawaiian riding dress was male attire. Bird took this as a serious and personal attack on her image and reputation and wrote angrily to Murray about it.

Isabella Bird to John Murray III, 16 Oakley Square, London, 21 November 1879

Dear Mr Murray

I am exceedingly annoyed with the exaggerations and mistakes in the Times notice of my book but these cannot be helped. More than all I am annoyed and justly with the statement that I 'donned masculine habiliments'. It is simply horrible and a lady ought to be protected from such truly 'libellous' treatment on the part of reviewers.

Can the enclosed note be inserted if the book should go into a second edition which possibly it may?

Yours very sincerely

Isabella L. Bird

Note to the second edition

~~In consequence of a misapprehension on the part of the Times and other critics, and~~ For the benefit of other lady travellers, I wish to explain that my 'Hawaiian riding dress' is the 'American Lady's Mountain Dress', a half-fitting jacket, a skirt reaching to the ankles, and full Turkish trousers gathered into a band with a frilling over the boots, a thoroughly serviceable and feminine costume for mountaineering and other rough travelling, as in the Alps or any part of the world.

I. L. B.

The next edition of *A Lady's Life in the Rocky Mountains* carried her note and an illustration of her in costume. This image became a feminist icon and was used by suffragettes on their banners.

Through her writing Isabella attempted to justify her life of daring travel, addressing personal and societal concerns over the propriety and usefulness of her journeys. In this she enjoyed only limited success. The distinguished Assyrian archaeologist Sir Austen Henry Layard was appalled on reading her *Journeys in Persia and Kurdistan* (1891), writing to Hallam Murray on 4 January 1892: 'I have only read a few of the opening chapters of Mrs Bishop's book . . . I must say that I think a woman must be devoid of all delicacy and modesty who could travel as she did, without a female attendant, among a crowd of dirty Persian muleteers & others. Had there been an imperative act of duty or some great end in view it might have been different, but as far as I can gather she had no object but to satisfy her curiosity & love of travel.'

A LADY'S LIFE

IN THE

ROCKY MOUNTAINS

By ISABELLA L. BIRD,

AUTHOR OF 'SIX MONTHS IN THE SANDWICH ISLANDS,' ETC. ETC.

WITH ILLUSTRATIONS

FOURTH EDITION

LONDON: JOHN MURRAY, ALBEMARLE STREET

1881

[*The right of translation is reserved.*]

Isabella's growing reputation as a traveller resulted in her being elected a founding member of the Royal Scottish Geographical Society (RSGS) in 1884. Six years later, the Royal Geographical Society (RGS), based in London, invited her to address them on her return from Tibet, but she refused to address a society that would not admit her as a fellow. Instead, on 31 May she talked at the RSGS London branch's second meeting. In response the RGS granted reciprocal rights to female members of other geographical societies, including the RSGS, and in July it agreed to admit female fellows to the RGS. Isabella, nominated by John Murray IV, was part of the first cohort of female nominees and she was elected in December 1892. This agitated a vocal minority of senior figures, including Murray's author Admiral Francis Leopold McClintock and Lord Curzon, and a private and public debate on the role of women in the society ultimately rejected any further women fellows. The twenty-two who had been admitted, Isabella among them, were allowed to remain. It wasn't until 1913 that the RGS finally admitted female fellows on a permanent basis.

Isabella Bird to John Murray IV, Tobermory, Isle of Mull, 4 December 1892

Dear Mr Murray

Let me at once thank you for so kindly informing me of my admission to the RGS. It is very pleasant that you were my proposer. I have not received any official intimation of my election though according to the Rules the Secretary should have made one.

So far the winter here remains exceptionally fine and I am able to go out on horseback for an hour daily which I find beneficial and my general health has certainly improved.

I am very sorry to hear that Mr Hallam Murray has been ill again. I doubt if rheumatism ever lets go its grip of its victims. I hear that the Riviera is very cold this winter.

41 Morningside Park
Edinburgh
Feb 19/93

I really must send the foregoing lines old as they are with an explanation that rheumatic gout in my right hand for many weeks made writing impossible. On Friday I had the pleasure of a long consultation with Miss Murray at Lord Kinnaird's and am glad to be placed once more en rapport with your family. It is a very happy arrangement for your sisters that Mr Hallam Murray is living at Wimbledon. The life there without the brightness which Mr Murray shed round him must have been a trying one.

I was intending to write to say with what pleasure I have noticed that many of Mr Murray's literary friends are rallying around you, and that in spite of the alleged love of the public for 'snippets' your list carries on the old traditions of the house. I should think that you certainly have no need for anxiety about the future.

Edward Whymper has been doing some beautiful illustrations for me of Lesser Tibet. Do look at them if you happen to see the Leisure Hour for March.

I am still very much out of health and do not think of going to England till the end of April.

With much kind regards to Mrs Murray
Believe me
Yours sincerely
Isabella Lucy Bishop

Isabella Bishop, née Bird, to John Murray IV, Kensington, Eastbourne, 27 May 1893

Dear Mr Murray

I have received the enclosed which is I suppose the circular of which you were speaking to Mr Kiltie. I don't care to take any steps in the matter as I never took any regarding admission. Fellowship as it stands at present is not a distinction, and not a recognition of work and really is not worth taking any trouble about. At the same time, the proposed action is a dastardly injustice to women.

Have you seen the article upon it in the Westminster Gazette of today? I am sorry that the editor has used my name in order to point or make an invidious remark on 'the Admirals'!

If you have time will you write and tell me the result of Monday's meeting. I am going to Lambeth Palace for a few days on Thursday, and then to Sir Alfred Lyall's.

Kind regards to Mrs Murray

Yours very sincerely

Isabella L. Bishop

Isabella enclosed the following letter from Douglas William Freshfield, the secretary (afterwards president) of the Royal Geographical Society, 26 May 1893.

Dear Madam,

The Associated Fellows have given notice that they will take steps at the Anniversary Meeting on Monday next at 2.30 p.m. at the University of London to ensure the removal of all Lady Fellows from the Society. It is desirable you should send your friends to prevent any such proceeding and support the new Council List.

Yours faithfully

Douglas W. Freshfield

Isabella Bishop, née Bird, to John Murray IV, Eastbourne, 6 June 1893

Dear Mr Murray

By your handwriting on a letter received this morning re-addressed from Lambeth Palace, I see that I forgot to send you my address, which I now enclose. I returned on Saturday evening.

I am going to meet Mr Curzon at the RGS on Tuesday or Wednesday regarding a subject on which he can give me some helpful information, and afterwards unless it be too late I should like to accept Mrs Murray's kind invitation to 'look in' at lunchtime.

I am amazed to see that Mr Freshfield both in a circular and in a letter to Saturday's Times has referred to my declining to read a paper in the RGS in an inaccurate way, which makes me ridiculous. My health was breaking down at the time, and I could not prepare a paper and I added in declining in a friendly note these words as nearly as possible: It seems scarcely consistent in a society which does not recognise the work of women to ask a woman to read a paper.

I never made any claim to be 'a geographer', and I hope that none of my friends have ever made it for me. As a traveller and observer I have done a good deal of hard and honest work, and may yet do more, but I never put forward any claim to have even that recognised by the RGS. If I had thought that any use would be made of my note I should not even have written the above remark.

I have not seen Mr Curzon's letter to which Mr Freshfield's seemed a (not very tactful) reply.

I think it might be well if ladies were ejected as it would tend to a reconsideration of the qualifications for fellowship, and possibly to a move in the direction of having <u>membership</u> as a matter of election and subscription and fellowship as a <u>distinction</u>.

Yours sincerely

Isabella L. Bishop

The friendship and support of John Murray III started with the publication of her first book in 1856, and continued with his sons, until her death in 1904. Following a near half-century of friendship, her recollection on the death of John Murray III in 1892 was one of the most touching received by the family: 'I made Mr Murray's acquaintance as a young girl, and in all this time have never received anything from him but the utmost kindness and consideration as well as sympathy in such of my affairs as I ventured to trouble him with. Thoughts of kindness and help, of giving pleasure to others, seemed to come so naturally to him, and made him so loveable. Just a year ago he wrote me such a kind note asking me to meet Mr Gladstone. How his geniality, brightness, and enjoyment of the society of his friends, and the way in which he made people acquainted with each other, made those gatherings in Albemarle Street, as Mr Gladstone said, "the most charming in London". How many must remember them as I do, and the dear figure which, no matter who was there, was always the central one. So true and loyal a friend will leave so very large a vacant place.'

26

Man and Superman
George Bernard Shaw

——•——

Irish playwright, critic and political activist George Bernard
Shaw wrote over sixty plays, establishing a reputation for his
publications and performances. One of his most renowned
works was *Man and Superman* (1902), a controversial four-act
philosophical drama based on the Byronic *Don Juan* theme,
which, given its sensitive nature, was an unusual work for the
playwright to propose to Murray's.

George Bernard Shaw to John Murray IV, Adelphi Terrace,
22 May 1903

Dear Sir

Would you care to publish my latest book? It is already
printed; and I am prepared to make a commission arrangement (if you prefer it) so that you shall not run any risk; but
before I send you a copy I should like to know how –
assuming that you are acquainted with my literary position
– you feel as to the desirability of publishing for me on any
terms. The book, I may say, is an almost excessively characteristic one, and will certainly not escape a good deal of
notice of a mixed kind.

I wish to change my current publishing arrangements
because the business of my present publisher is, in my

opinion, gradually developing off my lines. The separation is quite a friendly one.

I want to publish late in June or in July, or at all events in time to get the book noticed before the rising of parliament. For various reasons this is the best time for me.

Yours faithfully

G. Bernard Shaw

Murray replied immediately that he would need to see the book to consider it.

George Bernard Shaw to John Murray IV, Adelphi Terrace,
2 June 1903

Dear Sir

Thank you for your letter of the 22nd of May. Since then I have been waiting for a set of corrected proofs from the printer.

I was not so unreasonable as to expect you to publish a book without reading it – though I must say my normal grievance is that the publisher will <u>not</u> read my MS, and comes to me six months after publication full of the unexpected news that the book, which he has just looked at for the first time, is quite interesting. But my position is a rather more difficult one. No publisher or editor will tell me flatly that he won't publish anything of mine (because of his Church connextion, or Nonconformist connextion, or whatever it may be): he says he will be happy to consider anything I send him. I always take this as a polite form of refusal. To save loss of time and misunderstanding I have to find out first whether the field is really open; and that was the object of my previous letter.

Will you now do me the favour to read the book
yourself? A professional reader cannot help you in this
matter, as the mere question of literary presentability has
been settled long ago in my case. You do not, I presume,
want to pay someone to tell you that I am a 'paradoxical &
brilliant writer', and all the rest of the clichés about me.
But the character of the book is very considerably under
question. It deals with the most controversial questions,
with the most delicate subjects; and there are people who
will forgive John Murray for Byron who won't forgive
John Murray for this. Perhaps I am making too much of
the affair: indeed, I hope I am. But I may not have carried
off the dangerous passages quite so cleverly as I suppose;
and I therefore, even at the risk of overdoing it, beg you
not to touch the book on anyone else's recommendation,
but to read it yourself.

I enclose sheets B to P inclusive. Sheet A, which I will
send when it arrives (probably tomorrow or the next day)
consists of a long preface in the form of an epistle dedica-
tory to A. B. Walkley, who suggested the play to me – 'a
Don Juan play' was what he proposed. He has read the
dedication, and consents willingly to its publication. Sheet
P will contain a set of aphorisms in the manner
of La Rochefoucauld. These will also follow presently.
So the public cannot complain of scant measure for their
money.

I am anxious to know your decision because I want to
publish before parliament rises; and I want to find an
American publisher. American publishers are very timid; and
if I can send the book as accepted by John Murray for
England it will perhaps save me the trouble and expense of

having the book printed in America at my own expense &
formally published in time to save the copyright.

Yours faithfully

G. Bernard Shaw

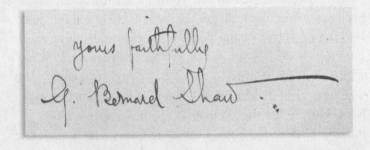

Murray sent a thoughtful and detailed rejection on 9 June 1903,
stating that he had been 'much interested and in parts amused
by it' and responding to Shaw's request for 'a personal opinion,
on the question of publication, and this I will give . . . always
assuming that you wish me to deal with you as frankly as you
have dealt with me'. Murray turned down the chance to publish
as 'The object of the book is to cast ridicule upon – or perhaps
I shall say to assail – marriage and other social & religious
institutions. Now however much a man may disapprove of these
institutions it seems to me that respect for the very deep-seated
feelings which hundreds of thousands of educated people entertain in regard to them should induce them to make the attack
in a somewhat reverent form: setting forth the arguments on
both sides and stating clearly what is to be the substitute &
how it is to be attained. In such cases as these, I venture to
think that the argument from ridicule will not touch the
thoughtful and tends to do more harm than good among
the thoughtless. I daresay you will say that I am old-fashioned
& conventional; I am fully prepared to accept the description.

However imperfectly I may express my meaning I write from a very sincere conviction for which I am sure you will make all proper allowance. At least I am equally sincere in again thanking you for having consulted me in this matter.' To this considered response, Shaw replied the next day.

George Bernard Shaw to John Murray IV, Adelphi Terrace,
10 June 1903

Dear Sir

I am greatly obliged to you for reading 'Man and Superman' so promptly, and for the memorandum of errors. Also – and this more deeply – for your friendly treatment of me.

I am sorry, being an incorrigible preacher, that the book has no message for you. I assure you that there is in it what is to me a perfectly serious religion, a perfectly practicable and urgently needed policy, a view of heaven and hell that is quite real, and a criticism of life that drives most modern men either to what I have depicted as hell, or to the pessimism of Ecclesiastes. I propose a tertium quid.

You say I should punch an Archbishop's head reverently because hundreds of thousands of educated people regard him with awe. But if I am to take their point of view, why punch his head at all? Of course I <u>could</u> do it reverently. Since my opinion of marriage is that of the apostles, I could express it in the words of St Paul instead of making Don Juan call it 'the most licentious of human institutions'. I could, without rousing the slightest suspicion of Nietzschianism, convey my opinion of morality by the un-exceptionable remark that righteousness is filthy rags. I am, like you, an old-fashioned and conventional man, confronted by a mass of stupidity, ignorance, want of social conscience, rationalism, materialism, and lascivious aestheticism. Nothing easier then for me to save unpleasantness (since I have 'independent' income) by saying my need in the old-fashioned phrases which nobody now understands. But I am afraid you would object just as strongly to a string of platitudes as to a string of blasphemies. And my business is to shock people into thinking, not to soothe them into apathy. I am an assayer of people's beliefs; and I have to do it with hydrochloric acid, not with sugar and water. Do you remember what Newman said when they told him that he should try to be controversial without being offensive: 'I have tried it,' he said; 'and nobody listened to me.' Profiting by his experience, I have never tried it, and don't intend to. As to ridicule, I value it above most social solvents. The world has not been particularly reverent to my convictions; and I am extremely obliged to it, as it has refined them continually by that process.

You must read Man & Superman again in ten years' time. It proposes as well as exposes. Again, sincere thanks.

Yours faithfully

G. Bernard Shaw

In addition to the immediate appreciation of Murray's considerate rejection, four decades later Shaw still admired his manner, writing to the publisher Daniel Macmillan, on 11 September 1943, that 'John Murray's Byronic prestige was so select that I did not dream of trying him until years later, when I was an author of some note and had already helped to bankrupt three publishers. I offered Man & Superman. He refused in a letter which really touched me.'

27

'It has been a task of no ordinary difficulty'
The Letters of Queen Victoria

———◆———

Following Queen Victoria's death in 1901, the unusual decision was made to publish a selection of her private correspondence, the first time any sovereign of England's correspondence would appear in print. A. C. Benson, who was considered the unofficial Poet Laureate and responsible for writing 'Land of Hope and Glory' as a coronation ode for King Edward VII in 1902, was appointed co-editor, with royal courtier Lord Esher as co-editor and manager for the publication of *The Letters of Queen Victoria, 1837–1861* (1907). Faced with the complexities of selecting, editing and printing the correspondence, theirs was a challenging task. Princess Beatrice, acting as Victoria's literary executor, had her own strong views on how the Queen should be portrayed, insisting on presenting her as a formal head of state, while Edward VII, who had to approve the proofs, showed little interest in reading them and was frequently out of the country, often taking the waters at Baden-Baden, Marienbad and elsewhere. As the first volume was already in proof and about to be printed, the princess decided additional correspondence must be added, thereby requiring last minute efforts to incorporate them. Six people were involved with the proofs, with six different ideas as to how to treat them. All agreed, however, that Victoria should be shown in a regal and imperial light, rather than as a woman or mother.

*A. C. Benson to John Murray IV, Tremans, Horsted Keynes,
12 August 1906*

<u>Private</u>

My Dear Murray

Many thanks to you for your letters & enclosure which is extremely satisfactory; & I am very grateful to you for all your kindness & care.

As to the Queen's Letters, I can <u>well</u> understand your feeling. The delay is intolerable. I can't tell you what personal inconvenience it is causing me, as I was counting on getting the book more or less complete before term began again, & I can only say that I have done my best to move matters. I have written very strongly to Esher, & several times. If he is vexed with me for my impertinence, & shows the letters to HM the fat is in the fire.

I will tell you formally & confidentially that I am meditating a final coup — withdrawing from the editorship. If much objection is taken to what we have done, & if much rearrangement &c becomes necessary, I think I shall say plainly that I will have nothing more to do with it. Of course it would mean throwing away some money &c — but it will give them some idea of how the delays irritate one. Royalty have no conception how much trouble they give & no one ever tells them. It is not want of consideration so much as a deplorable kind of education they receive.

I have mentioned this as yet to no one but yourself; but if I can't get things to move, I shall write to Esher in the same sense shortly. Please regard this as wholly confidential.

Ever yours
A. C. B.

With so many people involved and so many contrary views, publication of the letters proved a nightmare, but it brought enormous prestige to Murray's and eventually John Murray IV and V were knighted for their services. The book also brought problems, however. The Times Book Club wanted to discount it heavily to its members, but Murray's refused to supply it at less than the full price of three guineas. Murray IV was then accused by a *Times* reviewer of extortion and was compared to Judas Iscariot. Murray subsequently sued for libel and was awarded £7,500 damages. In November 1908 Murray's and *The Times* co-published a cheap edition of the letters.

28

The Story of San Michele
Axel Munthe

———•———

Murray's first publication by Swedish doctor Axel Munthe was *Letters from a Mourning City* (1887), a harrowing account of cholera sufferers in Naples, whom he rushed to help when he heard of their plight. This was followed by the quirky and meditative collection of short stories, *Memories and Vagaries* (1898), and his reminiscences of his time in the ambulance corps, *Red Cross, Iron Cross* (1916), that enjoyed modest acclaim, but all were overshadowed by his semi-autobiographical *The Story of San Michele* (1929), named after his eclectic and beautiful house, built on the site of an ancient villa on Capri. The book enjoyed extraordinary sales internationally, with Munthe generously donating all his profits to animal charities. With deteriorating eyesight, his letters were typewritten in an attempt at greater legibility, but this was seldom achieved.

Axel Munthe to John Murray V, Anacapri, Bay of Naples,
1 October 1930

My dear John Murray – your father wanted me to call him so and I hope hos son will agree yo yje same.

I suppose you will be back in your famous office by now after your well earned rest. . Dutto n has just sent me his edition of ?e, and vagaries, you ought to send him at once the new preface to this book fory je nex impression if any. he also sendz me the S Michele with its ' new prefac for the American edition' . if he is to publish the ed Cross I make a condition that its new preface is included without which I do not ayc-torize an american edition. Sice my return ha rly a day has passed without the most amazing letters from unk own amerocan admirers of S Michelle, doctors, bishops , authors and mote of or less exuberant ladies The American ambassador to Rome- thinl to:d y ou I had lent him S _ ichelle — says that n his lifetime no new book has had such a success in his country , He is an intelligent and learned man, he is siad to possess one of the finest libraries in America. . Sevenuch publishers are still foghtong for the dutch copyright , have now left ot to Bonnier t make the choice. In Germany they are b now eight and I am giving the preference to a Leipzog firm who wrote that they are certain of the success in Germany will exceed the English success , he sug suggests an illustrated edition but I am against it Bonnier has sold sixteen thousand copies in five months . an unique recors in Sweden/ Al Michel in paris wants to publish the book at once but I have declined until the French translation is improved. The xanish and fonnish editi are in the press. Here Fratelli Treves of Milan, the best known firm in Italy is full of prise and predicts great success In Sweden they are talki ng a lot about the nobel prize laso in America , but his is abso;utely excluded also because the eighteen members of th acade who are to give the prize are nearly all futurists and besides green withe envy and they cannot forgive a swede for having written in english. How are you getting on witn the warbool? it will sell but iy will prove flat to most readers after the S Michele. So wil. the Mem a Vagaries . had it not been fprt yjr mpney I would not have consented to their re publication. As usual I s;eep less well here than in London I am so depressed and wretched that life is not worth living. I see les less and less, readi ng is now finished My kind regards to your wife and to Lord G and to Farquharson is S Michele still selling? The editor of th Spectator has written and begged me to write an artic for his Cmas number but I have answered that I have nothing to say

Yours Axel Munthe

Munthe wrote to John Murray V in January 1929 about Murray's book manager and editor: 'Mr Farquharson has been amazingly patient and wide awake about it, you have got the right man in the right place there.' He took an interest in Farquharson's health, recommending specific medicines and regularly suggesting he play golf to relax from the pressures of publishing. However Munthe also harangued him frequently, complaining about editorial interference with his text and maintaining a completely unrealistic expectation of how quickly his work could be taken through the publishing process. For example he protested that the Queen of Sweden was having problems getting his books from a bookseller in Baden Baden, Germany: 'my patient, the Queen of Sweden, is very angry, though you do not care a D— about it, being the red little anarchist you are.' The following is a typical letter.

Axel Munthe to William Farquharson, Torre di Materita, Capri, 13 November 1930

Dear Mr Farquharson

I am very angry with you, I have been accustomed for thirty years that those I give my advice follow them. I know more about your body than you do and I tell you again to go to the dentist Cross at Buckingham Road and tell him from me that we are anxious to keep you in good condition and that it is absolutely essential that you can masticate your food properly. Actually you gulp it down like a dog. Part of your trouble has to do with ill-digested food. I have always suspected you were an obstinate little man, but I do not know that you were not clever enough to realize that I know what I am talking about. To put your teeth in order is more important than for you to play golf. Please have a copy of San Michele, last edition, sent to Mr Antonio Pastor, the Athenaeum Club, Pall Mall, with the author's compliments and a copy of the Red Cross and the Vagaries to Sir Rennell

Rodd, 39, Bryanston Square. I have given the Dutch copyright to Becht of Amsterdam, I think at least a dozen Dutch publishers have been asking for it. There is now also to be a Polish translation. Please also send a copy of the Red Cross to the Hon. Maud Ritchie, 8 Walton Place, Hans Place and a copy of the Vagaries to Miss Newton, 49, Eaton Terrace and a copy of the Red Cross to Lady Juliet Duff. Her address is in the telephone book, I believe it is Bedford Belgrave Square and a copy of both Red Cross and Vagaries to Mrs Crawshay, 75, Upper Berkeley Street. Kind greetings to the Colonel and Lord Gorell.

I forgot to beg you to send a copy of the Red Cross to Lady Oxford, Bedford Square, 44.

Yours

A. M.

See that the right books are sent to the right people.

29

'I cannot believe a word of it'
Film Rights

As the twentieth century progressed new opportunities and challenges arose for publishers in the area of film rights. Silent films grew in popularity in the late 1920s, but the introduction of talking films created a new level of interest, especially in France, Britain and the United States of America. One of the highest profile films of the silent era was a British film based on the life of Murray's author David Livingstone, of which Murray became a shareholder and promoter.

The Livingstone Film Expedition to John Murray IV, 86 Pall Mall, London, 13 October 1923

Dear Mr Murray

The outstanding address given by the Rt. Hon. Viscount Burnham at the farewell luncheon, Hotel Victoria, has aroused considerable interest in the expedition which is about to leave for Central Africa to film the life and work of the celebrated explorer, David Livingstone.

A number of friends have been kind enough to favour me with messages of goodwill, which will be published in our brochure prior to their departure on the 19th instant.

We wish to make this as representative as possible as in the judgement of Lord Burnham this is, 'a National Enterprise'.

Therefore, if you could favour us with a few words of encouragement we should consider it indeed of great value, and it would further the cause that Livingstone had so much at heart.

Yours faithfully

J. Aubrey Rees

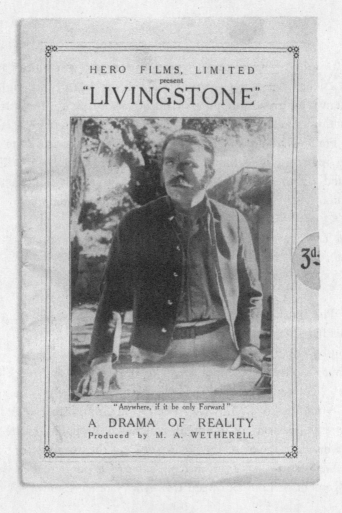

HERO FILMS, LIMITED
present
"LIVINGSTONE"

"Anywhere, if it be only Forward"

A DRAMA OF REALITY
Produced by M. A. WETHERELL

Although P. C. Wren wrote over thirty novels, he is best known for those based on the French Foreign Legion, the most notable success being *Beau Geste* (1924), which sold 84,000 copies in its first year and had been translated into fifteen languages by 1938. It was also filmed three times, in 1926, 1939 and 1966, and televised in 1982–4. Murray's manager William Farquharson advised P. C. Wren, on 19 September 1925, that the American motion picture company Famous Players-Lasky Corporation had agreed a $5,000 advance, on a payment of $22,500, for the *Beau Geste* film rights. Wren replied by telegram in disbelief that such a large sum was on offer.

P. C. Wren to William Farquharson, 20 September 1925

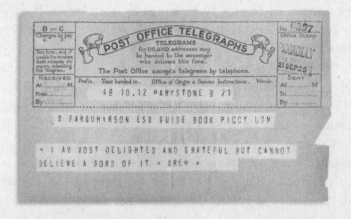

Unfortunately, Wren was right to be sceptical. On 25 September 1925 Farquharson replied: 'I must say I have been rather excited over the recent film deal, but I too, like you, had a feeling in my mind that it was too good to be true, and, alas it is so! We have just discovered that the book was not copyrighted in America, and so the Famous Lasky people will not pay such a high price. We have the 5,000 dollars, and without doubt we shall keep that . . . This is extremely disappointing.'

Murray V, however, didn't hold a grudge over the lost film rights and welcomed the promotional opportunities of the film itself. As Wren was unwell at the London premiere Murray was asked to represent his author, who supplied this speech, including his humorous additional final comment in which he proudly refers to his printed list of books as his godchildren.

P. C. Wren to John Murray V, 1 November 1926

Speech, Piccadilly Hotel: I consider myself extraordinarily fortunate in having my book filmed by the Famous Players-Lasky Productions, and extraordinarily unfortunate that I cannot be present tonight to express my satisfaction.

When the Wages of Virtue appeared, I was reported dead, although moderately alive, and now that BEAU GESTE makes its first appearance in England, I am reported alive, but feel moderately dead.

The story of BEAU GESTE has been termed 'the romance of a generation', but a much greater romance is in the story of its filming, an account which reads like a fairy tale. The story of BEAU GESTE has been said to contain impossibilities. The story of the filming of BEAU GESTE does contain impossibilities, or rather would do so, if there were such things as impossibilities for the Famous Players-Lasky Organisation.

I too would like to hope for a further impossibility – that BEAU GESTE might make the Famous Players-Lasky even more famous than they are.

By a curious and pleasing coincidence, today, November 1st is my birthday, as well as that of the BEAU GESTE film in England. I wish many Happy Returns to the Plaza; many Happy Returns of every spectator of the film; and enormous Happy Returns from the box office to the Famous Players-Lasky Organisation.

[annotated in pencil by John Murray V] One word more – Major Wren has not forgotten his good wishes to those gathered here this evening and asks you to accept a special copy of his book. If you will turn to the back of the title page you will find a table of the dates when my godchildren came into being – isn't it a wonderful record.

Murray related the success of the day to Wren: 'The excitement opened before midday, when crowds began to collect at the Plaza. When I happened to go along there at lunchtime, there was a long queue stretching down Regent Street one way, and down Jermyn Street the other way, and for the first performance, hundreds were turned away. There was quite a lot of excitement, as they had got men dressed up in the Legion uniform at the doors and on the balcony. At the dinner, I was the guest of the evening, as representing you. It was a great success. Your message pleased the Lasky people very much, particularly the ending, and it had a good reception with the guests. I prefaced it with a few words, and I send you a typed copy of them, as I thought you might like to know what I said. The last paragraph marked in blue, was Colonel Murray's [JM V] suggestion, and you will note his rather witty play upon words! There were ladies present, and I was a little in doubt as to the propriety of ending thus, but the joke was well received – in fact I think the ladies enjoyed it more than the men! I ended your message by asking each of the guests to accept a special autographed copy of your book with your good wishes. In these copies I had inserted your photograph, with an inscription taken from one of your letters to me (as enclosed) and these were very much appreciated, and I think the idea was a bit of good publicity. Of course, we bear the cost of these copies. After dinner we went on to the Plaza, and I enjoyed the film very much indeed, and am so pleased that they kept so closely to the book. It is a wonderful production. I also enclose the menu, and a programme, as I thought you might like to have these.'

In addition to film rights there was a lucrative trade in radio rights and Wren and Murray accepted an offer of $1,000 for a one-hour dramatisation during the Campbell Soup Hour on the NBC network. The radio play was first broadcast on 17 March 1939 starring Laurence Olivier as John Geste and Orson Welles as his brother Michael 'Beau' Geste.

The success of *The Story of San Michele* also sparked interest among American film companies, Paramount for example offering $30,000 for the movie rights. However, Munthe was reluctant to be involved in any film deal, as were Murray's, despite frequent requests from E. P. Dutton, their American counterpart, whose managing director wrote persistently to Farquharson.

John MacRae to Walter Farquharson, New York, USA, by
Cablegram, 14 March 1931

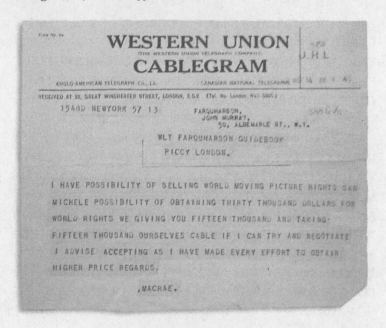

I HAVE POSSIBILITY OF SELLING WORLD MOVING
PICTURE RIGHTS SAN MICHELE POSSIBILITY OF
OBTAINING THIRTY THOUSAND DOLLARS FOR WORLD
RIGHTS WE GIVING YOU FIFTEEN THOUSAND AND
TAKING FIFTEEN THOUSAND OURSELVES CABLE IF I CAN
TRY AND NEGOTIATE I ADVISE ACCEPTING AS I HAVE
MADE EVERY EFFORT TO OBTAIN HIGHER PRICE
REGARDS
   MACRAE

John MacRae to Walter Farquharson, New York, USA, by Cablegram, 31 March 1931

PARAMOUNT PICTURE PEOPLE DESIROUS OF GETTING
DECISION ON PICTURE RIGHTS MUNTHES SAN MICHELE
THEY NOW PROPOSE ROYALTY ON GROSS SALES THREE
PERCENT TO FIRST MILLION DOLLARS FOUR PERCENT
ON SECOND MILLION DOLLARS FIVE PERCENT ON ALL
GROSS SALES OVER TWO MILLION ADVANCE OF
TWENTYFIVE HUNDRED DOLLARS ON ACCOUNT OF
ROYALTY I HAVE ADVISED PARAMOUNT PICTURE PEOPLE
TO HAVE THEIR LONDON AGENT CALL AND DISCUSS THIS
MATTER WITH YOU PERSONALLY PLEASE SEE THIS MAN
AND GIVE THE MATTER THAT CAREFUL CONSIDERATION
WHICH IT REQUIRES IT WOULD BE A PITY TO LOSE THE
MONEY FROM MOVING PICTURE RIGHTS PARAMOUNT
PEOPLE SAY THEY WILL NOT WAIT FOR MY DECISION I
LEAVE THE MATTER TEMPORARILY IN YOUR HANDS.
    MACRAE

A letter followed.

John MacRae to William Farquharson, New York, USA, 15 April 1931

Dear W. Farquharson

    Thank you for your gracious, kindly note of April 7th. I observe that Dr Munthe does not want to act decisively in the matter of the moving picture of THE STORY OF SAN MICHELE. I can quite understand his feelings in the matter and can sympathize with him. Strictly and confidentially speaking, between two practical men of considerable experience in the book world, these moving pictures people in the United States have arrived at a point where they might be properly classed with the old robber barons who built their castles along the Rhine. Sometimes when I discuss moving pictures with this amalgamated crowd, I feel that I would like to bluntly refuse every kind of offer they make. What these people want, is to buy the finest pearl necklace at the price of plain ordinary Indian beads. I feel it my duty to transmit to you the various offers made to us for the moving picture of THE STORY OF SAN MICHELE. As it were, I have now left the matter in the lap of the gods, namely, in the hands of the author, who after all is entitled to do with it what he would like.

It is quite possible, that before these mobbing picture people get through, one of them will make a much better offer than has been made. Of course no moving picture people could have been bribed by giving them $100,000 to make an offer to make a moving picture of THE STORY OF SAN MICHELE, when it was first published by us or by you. THE STORY OF SAN MICHELE has those strange human elements within its loins and veins, which make it alive to people who read books. Because the book sells and people talk about it, it has kept the book moving in sale, these people will come back for the moving picture; if one doesn't take it another will.

I had a similar experience with Blasco Ibanez's THE FOUR HORSEMEN OF THE APOCALYPSE. For a long time these people ground their teeth and refused to offer more than $5,000. Finally, they raised their offer to $20,000; and at last I made them pay on a royalty basis. Blasco Ibanez received somewhere around $250,000.

I shall await with interest and perfect peace of mind whatever decision Dr Munthe and Murray's make in regard to the moving pictures. In the meantime my job is to try and keep the book selling; with the present commercial slump in America, this is a difficult problem. There would be no chance whatever of keeping this book going on selling, through anybody or any method of advertising, if there was not that strange, marvellous, human, vital, magnetic something in the book, which makes everyone who reads it exclaim: 'What a grand book.' On the other hand, if we did not keep hammering away with advertising and with every energy we know how to use, this book would quickly slip down into a very low ebb of sale.

I have a letter from Dr Munthe, saying he will take up the matter of the moving picture with you when he comes to London. I have a very much more important statement from him, that he is getting along splendidly with the new book. I gather and judge that Dr Munthe intends for you to publish the book in London, and intends that I should publish it over here.

Please present my warm regards to the Colonel and all at Albemarle Street, and with warm regard for yourself and the hope you are well, I am

Sincerely yours

John MacRae

President Dutton

Munthe, feeling harassed, typed a letter to Murray's.

Axel Munthe to John Murray V, Terra di Materita, Capri, April 1931

Thanks for your letter – I cannot decide anything about the film business until I know what is at stake and with whom I am dealing. There is ample time for settling this business by letter. As to Dutton's claim I consider it monstrous. Nothing but the much needed money from those animals could make me agree for a moment to submit to this vulgarisation of our book. Unless it's a big sum I shall follow my inclination to refuse. There are other things to be considered before accepting. For instance I, who have violently criticized Charcot for his public demonstrations in the Salpêtrière of hypnotic phenomena, could never accept a film taken from the chapters on hypnotism and the Salpêtrière. How do I know that they might not reproduce such scenes? I repeat that I do not wish to settle this question until I am in London and have received more information about it. This is also the advice of my friend Garrett, the American ambassador in Rome. Please write to Dutton that I wish to settle this business personally in consultation with you and that I expect to be in London at the end of April. I leave for Rome about the twelfth of April – tell Farquharson – and please address any mail to Villa Svezia from then until I go north. Please send me at Villa Svezia in a week's time, when you get this letter, a copy of Red Cross and IC [Iron Cross]. San Michele has become a regular pilgrimage for tourists, they drive there straight from the steamer. But none has succeeded in entering the old tower which makes them very angry. Saluti to Lord G and Farquharson.

Yours ever
Axel Munthe

Murray wrote to MacRae on 3 June 1931: 'In America you do things in a hurry, but Dr Munthe does not! . . . Unfortunately, a good deal of irritation has been caused by Dr Munthe feeling that he is hustled; so even though things seem to go slowly, we must altogether unhustle him now!!'

On 16 May 1931 Paramount withdrew its offer and not until 1962 did his remarkable story appear on film.

30

'Killed by correspondence'
John Betjeman

———— ·•·◆·•· ————

John Betjeman and John 'Jock' Murray VI met and became friends when students at Magdalen College, Oxford. In spite of the renewed family practice against publishing poetry, Jock Murray persuaded his uncle, John Murray V, to publish Betjeman's second book of poetry, *Continual Dew* (1937). He did so by agreeing to underwrite any losses with his eighteenth birthday gift of 100 Bovril shares as security. Although the title made a modest loss he was allowed to keep his shares. Betjeman went on to become Britain's most popular poet as well as an influential conservationist, writer on architectural affairs and the scourge of developers.

Continual Dew was designed with eccentric care, with illustrations by Osbert Lancaster and Hubert de Cronin Hastings, a cover by E. McKnight Kauffer and a centre spread on prayer-book paper. Betjeman obsessed over typefaces, printing ornaments and the binding. The title page used the visual pun of a dripping tap and Betjeman wrote to Jock: 'Here is the tap & a tracing with the way to draw the drips of water. You might make a test & see whether they fall from the outside or inside rim of the tap. Certainly not in the middle.' These and other details gave the book a unique originality.

John Betjeman to John Murray VI, Garrards Farm, Berkshire,
23 October 1937

Dear Jock

Thank you so much for the book with which I am delighted. Ted's cover is magnificent. Most appealing and agreeable contrast with the lovely black and gold inside. The gilt edges are lovely. So is the grey paper. Loveliest of all is the prayer book paper.

'If the amount of trouble and money that has been expended on the production of this undergraduate persiflage had instead been spent on some of our young poets, the publishers at least could be congratulated.' Anticipated notice from New Statesman and Nation. You might put that on the cards you intend to send out.

My dear Jock, I feel it unlikely that you will sell more than a dozen copies and I do appreciate the charity, for I can only call it that, which has made you publish the verse in so exquisite a style. You and Lord Gorell will get your reward in heaven.

Didn't I send you a whacking great list of friends on brown paper? I haven't got an address book and it was the best I could do. If I think of some more I will let you know. Let me have some cards and I will enclose them in my letters.

Will you send back, some time, the books from which some of the illustrations were taken.

It's Murray's Guide to Oxfordshire not London, that John Piper wants to borrow.

With many many thanks.

Yours till death

John B.

Murray, noting Betjeman's appreciation of the physical appearance of his books, delighted in sending the poet a red velvet edition of his *Collected Poems* (1958) presented in a Morocco leather box. Only three such editions were made, at the cost of £30 each: one for Murray himself, one for Betjeman and one for Queen Elizabeth II. In 1960 Betjeman was awarded the Queen's Medal for Poetry and in 1972 he was appointed Poet Laureate.

John Betjeman to John Murray VI, The Mead, Wantage, Berkshire, 25 December 1958

My Dear Jock

I've never seen anything quite so swish as that red velvet edition in its Morocco box except that which was in the long royal fingers on that terrifying occasion. No man ever had a kinder or more considerate publisher than you. All I've had from Collins is a bill for twenty-one pounds against some extra copies I ordered of Parish Churches. How different is <u>Mr Murray</u> who sends delicious wine as well as books, and in which we drank your health at lunch today. Of course next year there will be the reaction and I shall suffer contempt, neglect and frustration. But I can now always look back to a really thrilling moment of triumph and shall never forget your and everybody's generosity. God bless you, old boy.

Everyone here sends love as does
Your diffident author,
John B.

John Betjeman's popularity as a poet and his position as a leading advocate for architectural preservation meant that numerous people wrote to him – indeed, too many for him to cope with – so he implored Murray to help relieve the pressure. In the same letter he laments the development of Rivington Place, Shoreditch, which he had campaigned against.

John Betjeman to John Murray VI, London, 15 August 1962

Dear Jock

I'm having to cut down on my correspondence which has got quite out of hand and takes up the major part of every working day. Do you think that your dear little firm would undertake to open and answer all letters addressed to me care of you, and only send on those from particular friends? I enclose a typical annoying letter which arrived today, together with a suggested reply to it. Isn't it sad about Rivingtons.

Yours, John B.

Jock replied immediately that 'we are delighted to do anything in our power to defend you from time-wasters, and until your new secretary becomes more competent and more ingenious than we are, we will certainly open your post, deflecting any that are not genuine love letters.' He added in a postscript: 'We are delighted to think that even a "dear little firm" can do something to defend a major poet from minor worries, and how splendid to think that the time saved will be used for creative purposes.'

However, a few years later Betjeman was again writing to renew his plea for help with correspondence.

John Betjeman to John Murray VI, London, 1 September 1966

Dear Jock

Please could you get your firm to answer the letters that
come to me through you. Naturally, I will pay any
expenses. But the answers are 1) to thank very much on
my behalf for the kind letter or interesting letter as the
case may be. 2) If poems or prose is enclosed again to
thank but to say that I have made a firm rule never to
comment on other people's work because our work is like
our children and publishers and editors are the best judges.
This will rule out about ten letters a day I receive at the
moment through your firm and will give me some time to
write and think. I must point out to you that my ordinary
correspondence about buildings occupies at least half of
every day of my week which is why I beg you to have
mercy on
       John B.

As more years passed the problem became even worse, especially
after Betjeman's appointment as Poet Laureate.

John Betjeman, to John Murray VI, London, 25 February 1977

Dear Jock

You said on the telephone today that you would undertake to answer the letters that come to me through you. I
enclose some that have come in the last ten minutes. It is a
question really of whether you want me to remain alive or
prefer to see me go under killed by correspondence. I would
far sooner pay someone to do it on your behalf if you
cannot undertake it from Albemarle Street. The only thing I

don't want to see is any more readdressed letters. Here is a specimen form that could go out.

Yours ever

John B.

Murray annotated this letter with the comment that among these regular letters forwarded by the overwhelmed Betjeman were ones from the BBC and the *Sunday Times*, in which Jock might reasonably have thought Betjeman should have taken an interest.

31

War in the Middle East
Freya Stark

———◆———

Travel writer Freya Stark's proficiency in languages, including Arabic, Turkish and Persian, was invaluable during the Second World War when she joined the Ministry of Information as an expert on Arabia, working as a propagandist in Aden, Yemen and Egypt. She founded the Brotherhood of Freedom which attempted to build support for democracy and encourage pro-British sympathy. Stark's acknowledged expertise led to her being invited to deliver a lecture series on the Palestine question in the United States of America, and her friend General Archibald Wavell, later Viceroy of India, also asked her to work in India. Her frequent letters to John Murray VI provide a fascinating insight into her worldwide war experiences, as well as her close friendship with Murray, who delighted her by making her godmother to his son John Murray VII. Stark wrote about her life during the war in *Letters from Syria* (1942) and *East is West* (1945), as well as her autobiographical *Dust in the Lion's Paw* (1961) and two volumes of her letters: *Bridge of the Levant, 1940–43* (1977) and *New Worlds for Old, 1943–46* (1978).

Freya Stark to John Murray VI, Aden, 15 June 1940

My Dearest Jock

What days and nights we live in. We have been bombed

three times in ten hours and I am ashamed to say that it is the only thing lately that I have <u>really</u> enjoyed. The Italians say we are in ashes, but that is rather exaggerated. As a matter of fact it was a revelation how over fifty bombs could do so little damage. One must admit that there is something in the theory of race, else why should the Indians all panic and rush off and the Arabs behave with perfect dignity? Dear Jock you will be in it all, far worse than we – and that is not pleasant. Nothing in Europe is, just now, except the spirit of our men and allies. One goes to the news with a sickish feeling – but someday the luck will turn, if one can call that luck which is the centre of the souls of men.

You will be glad to fight. There is a strange liberation when once you have looked into the eyes of Death and know that, beyond the natural human panic and recoil, there is nothing to fear. The earth becomes your garden and pleasure ground for ever when once you know that it is easy to leave. There are two families of mankind, those who know this and those who don't, and I am glad to think that you are among the freemen.

Harold is here and it is so pleasant to have him. He is a much less volatile friend than Stewart, who just leaves me in an air raid and forgets that I exist. I don't mind being alone, but the absent-mindedness is what pains me: Doreen is having a baby in Egypt and no one knows when she can get back. I myself think we shall not be very long in clearing up this end.

Love to Diana and baby and the best of luck to you. May we once more sit and drink vermouth at Feltre.

Your

Freya

Freya Stark to John Murray VI, Cairo, 5 December 1940

My Dearest Jock

It is rather ridiculous – your last letter to arrive is August 9th! I would like to have something more recent in these days of destruction. It was a very nice letter, and a comfort to me. All one's true affections mean very much just now. Ever since the uprooting at Asolo, I have felt most strangely lonely as if all my foundations had been shaken, I mean the visible foundations that depend on human habitations and relationships. And to tell you the truth it is a heavy task to have to do anti-Fascist work when one feels it may have such grim results over there. One just goes on and tries not to picture things. I would give I don't know what to know my two old people safely out. I believe Italy will be captured by Germany very shortly.

Here all goes steadily and risingly optimistic. I have been down with my third attack of 'flu these four days, not going out of the house, but rising from my bed (a) to meet my young men's committee; (b) to meet my ladies committee (far more exhausting); (c) to give my weekly evening party; (d) to give lunch to a mixed Anglo-Egyptian party; (e) to give lunch to the Air Marshal and others – among them nice Colonel Bagnold who motors up sand dunes. All this makes influenza rather slow and I feel very old, worn and exhausted just temporarily (old possibly permanently, but one may resuscitate even from that).

I begin to fear that the war is going to elude Egypt after all and wish I had studied Greek instead of Arabic. Here we deal with nothing but the machinery while you are having

all the explosions. I hope they leave you and Diana safe, dear
Jock — may 1941 end well for us all.

    Much much love to you

    Your

    Freya

Freya Stark to John Murray VI, Mount Carmel, 1 September 1941

My Dearest Jock

How exciting the world is with all these comings and
goings! I shall be proud to godmother little John. What fun!
When the war is over I think I shall dedicate the remainder
of my life to my godchildren — three girls and two boys at
present. I shall either live in a village in England or in a
whitewashed villa in Greece — or of course both if you
provide me with the income. In the English village I should
like to keep the shop: that is the only way to have a finger
in everybody's pie unless you are squire or parson — and it
would be a much more amusing angle from the shop.

I have been amusing myself these idle mornings under
the pines counting the names of as many books as I can
remember reading and was surprised to find how difficult
it was to reach 850: I then counted the people I could
remember and reached 1,200 easily. I think biographies could
quite well put such a list in their appendices — one is very
much made by the books one reads after all.

I now have General Weygand on Muhammad Ali, which
has a secondary interest as it shows the depth of the general's
anti-British feelings even before the war. In the account of
the siege and fall of Missolonghi he <u>never mentions Lord
Byron</u>, in fact only gives one cursory reference in the whole
account of the Greek war. You would think the whole

history of the East Mediterranean was made by Napoleon. The most parochial nation in the world the French.

Heaps of love to little John and his mama and sister

Your affectionate

Freya

Freya Stark to John Murray VI, Baghdad, 16 April 1943

My Dear Jock

I found your very dear little note of November and one of 24 March asking me to write on Arab relations. I couldn't do that now: I am right inside them, with lots of emotion but no tranquillity – and it's quite impossible. If I could write a book it would be about a pre-war world in Italy, but I can't write anything till all this is over. I hope we may talk of all this: there is a plan to give me a week or so in London en route for America in August or September. I dare hardly promise it, even to myself!

Johnnie Hawtrey and I travelled 4,000 miles over one long stretch of gravel that represents the trans-Iranian road: it took us nineteen days. We did all this with numerous arguments as to who was to drive. Johnnie's opinion of my driving is terribly unflattering – but no quarrels, which shows how unlike he was to Gertrude (miaow) and it really was most restful: every sort of desert and never a bit of propaganda. Isfahan is just like a pale turquoise, sky, clouds, white-stemmed trees, faded painted houses with rickety dilapidated columns, and blue domes in the sky.

I am back now to numerous tangles as one always is, and have to tour the whole of my parish before it gets too hot.

Your

Freya

Freya Stark to John Murray VI, New York, 20 November 1943

Dearest Jock

I am going mad in New York shops – fantastically expensive but <u>delirious</u>. Luckily I have no excuses to buy more costumes, but even little lacy blouses can almost bankrupt one and as for underthings with lace tops . . . oh my!

I can't get over the exciting beauty of New York – the pencil buildings so high and far that the blueness of the sky floats about them; the feeling that one's taxis, and shopping, all go on in the deep canyon-beds of natural erosions rather than in the excrescences of human builders.

I am being doctored now for anaemia, low blood pressure and all the results of operations, and hope to start the tour in January: that will not take me back to London till May.

Much love to you all

Freya

Freya Stark to John Murray VI, Simla, India, 11 May 1945

Dearest Jock

This high blue air is reviving me already, though I think the poor old creature needs a year of it. The ineffable feeling of getting up in the morning when you like, knowing you can do just what you like with your day!

It still seems incredible that the Western half of the nightmare is over. All sorts of clouds still lowering but the end of the actual destruction leaves a sort of blessed stillness. My God – may it be the last war in our time.

Simla is fantastic, a bees' nest on top of several hills joined by ridges – all trees and the shoddiest houses. No style either in building or people: the most sordid mixtures of types, but

a vague Victorian atmosphere about it, and the best-looking
people are the rickshaw coolies although they do sit about
in rags. Felicity Wavell and I are in Squire's Hall, a small and
charming house in the grounds of Viceregal Lodge, all
balconies and windows, and the view sloping away and
bordered by the great hills when they show. Simla lies like a
<u>parure</u> of topazes high up under the stars at night. If one
isn't a great walker, it is a prison: so high and every walk
ending in a steep drop where the pines and the fields and
villages go steeply down to the hidden clefts that drain to
Sutlej: but if one could walk there would be endless days in
the hills. What happens to you now? I suppose you stay on
till the Japs are finished? But I can't think it will be very
long.

Love, dear Jock

Freya

Many years later, after a lifetime of travelling, friendship, correspondence and writing books, Freya wrote again to Jock.

Freya Stark to John Murray VI, Asolo, 16 June 1979

Dearest Jock

Your letter has come, most welcome, though I would like
better news of your health. What a lot of letters we have
written each other since first I stepped full of awe into that
Byron room! Two wars have passed over it and ever so many
journeys; and now we needn't worry much over what
happens to us, for no one can take from us 86 years (a few
less for you) of a very interesting life. People forget this
<u>permanence</u> of the good times. It makes one remarkably free.

I wish I could give this freedom to Costanza. There seems to be no sign of a cure, and I am sad not only for her but for Paolo and would gladly go to her in Turin but she is being kept strictly quiet with no emotion, and can neither read nor move. Surely one should be allowed a little pill and freedom?

Dear love, dearest Jock. I think of you all so often. And so grateful for the books coming towards me. Have got a little pony-riding meanwhile.

Love from

Freya

32

'He will answer to me as a gentleman'
Adrian Conan Doyle

———•———

Sir Arthur Conan Doyle wrote over a hundred books and was one of the best known authors of his generation, most famous for his novels and in particular his tales featuring his most enduring creation, the detective Sherlock Holmes. Conan Doyle's son Adrian was highly sensitive to any adverse comments from his father's literary critics and those who mocked his strongly held spiritualist beliefs. So, when Harold Nicolson was thought to have insulted him in a review of Murray's publication of John Dickson Carr's *The Life of Sir Arthur Conan Doyle* (1949), almost twenty years after his father's death, Adrian reacted strongly, writing to their mutual friend John Murray.

Adrian Conan Doyle to John Murray VI, Hotel El Minzah, Tangier, 16 February 1949

My Dear John

I have now received a number of the press cuttings, and am glad to know that the great majority have welcomed the book for the masterpiece that it is.

I agree with you about the Manchester Guardian. And I have sent them a letter for publication, that will fall, like the lash of a dog's whip, across the features of their 'self styled' literary critic, R. G. J.

I turn now to a subject of much more serious import. I refer, of course, to the insults levied at my father by that contemptible creature, Harold Nicolson.

So far as the oblique shafts at Dickson Carr's integrity are concerned, Carr must answer these for himself, and, for this purpose, I have sent him my copy of the Daily Telegraph.

But, not content with that, Nicolson has seen fit to use a most insulting terminology in his reference to my father and grandmother.

This is a thing I cannot tolerate from any living man, and I have therefore decided upon an irrevocable step.

In the case of the great majority of literary critics, vicious lies at the expense of the dead are committed; but, should they offend, I would have no address against them, inasmuch that the average critic is nothing more than a literary tradesman.

Nicolson, however, claims to be a gentleman, and will answer to me as a gentleman.

You will bear in mind, my dear John, that the law affords me no redress against insults levied at my great father; nor would a punch in the eye result in anything but a charge for 'Assault and Battery', in addition to the fact that such a measure would be entirely inadequate to the offence.

I have, therefore, decided, after due consideration, to challenge Nicolson, under the degrees of absolute privacy and silence that are respected by a gentleman in such an affair, to meet in France, and, there, to give me the satisfaction that I demand, with whatever weapons he may choose.

Now, I am perfectly serious in this matter. Three duels have been fought during the past five years, between both French and Italians, and, therefore, I see no reason why an Englishman should not summon up sufficient courage to meet an Irishman, in this final way.

I have no intention of involving you in this affair beyond one favour, that, as you know both parties, I will ask you to perform.

On a separate page, attached to this letter, you will find my challenge. Will you please ask Nicolson to call on you and read my challenge to him. I have written to him myself, and told him that I have asked you to convey a private message from me.

I have taken the precautionary step in order to avoid any possibility of Nicolson refusing my challenge, and earning a few extra guineas by turning the matter into a newspaper article.

With my cartel held by a third party, who is cognisant of all the facts, even Nicolson would be ashamed to shield behind publicity.

Enclosed, a typed copy of my letter to him, as distinct from my challenge that you will kindly read to him.

As soon as he tells you that he accepts – as accept he must – I will ask you, as a final favour, to contact Captain ASH, at 53, Dukes Avenue, Muswell Hill, N. 10 and inform him of Nicolson's acceptation, and give him Nicolson's address, so that he may call upon him.

Believe me, my dear friend, I do not take this serious step without due consideration. It cannot affect the destiny of a great book, and, whatever the result of the combat, it can and will be a warning to cheap-minded men to step warily in the art of insulting the memories of our fathers.

With best wishes
Adrian

P.S. Would you have the kindness to send a copy of the Nicolson review to my brother Denis, c/o Government House, MYSORE, India. My copy has gone to Dickson Carr.

P.P.S. Since writing the above, I have received a letter from a stranger enclosing a copy of a letter that he has sent to Nicolson. This speaks for itself, & I have had the enclosed copy made for you.

Adrian Conan Doyle was even more forceful in writing to Nicolson: 'such falsehoods could only emanate from a mean-minded, mean-spirited man, lacking completely in that sense of truth and in that nobility of purpose, that are the first tenets of a gentleman. Any coward can insult the dead father. I give you this opportunity to prove your manhood by crossing to France to meet the living son.'

Nicolson did not take the challenge too seriously, as his letter to Murray shows.

Harold Nicolson to John Murray VI, Neville Crescent, London, 1 March 1949

> Confidential. Secret. Not to be shown to anyone, and to be burnt before you read it.

Dear John-Jock

I feel that typewriters ought to have a fount of tiny print in which one writes those letters which are so secret that they ought not to be overheard and should therefore be whispered rather than typed. This is to acknowledge your letter of February 28th, enclosing a typewritten copy of a letter written in your hand to a man whose name apparently I must not mention, but who seems to be a Knight of the Round Table.

I do not quite understand all this need for mystification and cryptic utterance, and I will regret to my dying day that your loyalty to Galahad has prevented me from writing what would have been, I feel sure, a most engaging Marginal Comment.

The worst of being discreet to excess is that it arouses appalling suspicions, and the fact that Lancelot calls you John when all the normal world calls you Jock, is a mystery which seems to me to belong to Lyonesse and all that tiresome business about the Holy Grail.

Anyhow, I expect you are being very wise over the whole matter, and I am ready to fall in with your stratagem and to play the cat's cradle with you. I have therefore altered the word 'Jock' to the word 'John' and sent the letter off to Tintagel.

Yours ever
Harold

When sixty-six-year-old Nicolson wrote to Conan Doyle that 'I fear I have long passed the duelling age and cannot accept your proposal', Conan Doyle admitted to Murray: 'I am shocked, however, to hear that the fellow is a generation older than ourselves. I had imagined him to be a man of about 45.' Murray, during his mediation, while making Nicolson aware of the seriousness of the insult, also confessed to enjoying the secrecy of the correspondence: 'I cheer myself up with the thought that an intermediary in a remarkable affair of this kind, can justifiably hide behind the cloak of the need for secrecy, and sometimes it gives me a feeling that I have not had since I left school.'

Adrian Conan Doyle to John Murray VI, Tangier, 8 March 1949

My Dear John

This is to let you know that I have today received a reply from Harold Nicolson. In his reply he offers a manly apology for his misstatements about my father, and states that he will find an opportunity to publicly rectify the false impression that his words were likely to create. Under these circumstances, I shall accept his apology and rely upon his sense of honour to take the right steps in the matter.

I want you to know that I shall always cherish in my memory the salient fact that you stood by me in this affair.

Words are idle things, but I want you just to know that if there is anything that I can ever do for you, or for yours, then I shall be there heart and hand.

Yours
Adrian

Harold Nicolson wrote an apology in *The Spectator* and confessed to John Murray VI on 19 March 1949, 'Certainly I did not wish to hurt him, and he was justified in being so angry.'

33

'He writes like an angel'
Patrick Leigh Fermor

For many, Patrick Leigh Fermor was the outstanding travel writer of the twentieth century. Prone to procrastination and perfectionism, it is unlikely he would have been as productive without the extraordinarily patient and loyal friendship and encouragement of John Murray VI. Although normally living in Greece or travelling abroad, Leigh Fermor was still a central figure in Murray's circle, with regular correspondence between them, as well as letters from fellow writers and travellers, artists and critics regarding Paddy often arriving at No. 50.

⇢⇢⇢⇠⇠⇠

Jock Murray and Leigh Fermor first collaborated when the *Cornhill Magazine*, then owned by Murray's, published some of his essays, including his accounts of monastic life. These pieces interested Ian Fleming, author of the James Bond novels and a director of the Dropmore Press as well as a journalist with the Kemsley newspaper group, owners of the *Sunday Times*.

Ian Fleming to John Murray VI, Great James Street, London,
20 April 1951

Dear Jock Murray

Many thanks for your letter and for your very helpful

attitude towards our Dropmore Press project. I will now write and discuss details with Paddy Leigh Fermor and see if he can provide illustrations.

Yes, I have certainly seen the spring 'Cornhill' – one of the very best numbers of this fine quarterly, but I was sorry to see that Peter Quennell has relinquished the editorship and I am doubly dismayed to hear rumours that you may be ceasing publication at the end of this year.

Surely this cannot be so? It is the last quality literary magazine in England.

Are there any problems in connection with its publication over which this group of newspapers with all our various facilities could help?

Yours ever

Ian Fleming

Murray agreed to the articles being reprinted by Dropmore, under the Queen Anne Press imprint, who produced a limited and beautifully illustrated edition of *A Time to Keep Silence* (1953), with Jock advising Fleming to 'pay him as much as you can, because mules are very expensive in Greece and apparently eat a lot'. Murray also published an edition, in 1957, with illustrations by John Craxton, who adored working on his friend's books, among them his first volume on Greece, *Mani: Travels in the Southern Peloponnese* (1958). Craxton wrote to Murray on 5 August 1958: 'Paddy's book-jackets are important in that they set a visual overture – I hope I have got the spirit of Paddy's amazing poetic clarity, he really is an incredible writer.' Following publication, he replied to Murray's praise of his work.

John Craxton to John Murray VI, Finchley Road, London,
8 November 1958

Very Dear Jock

Thank you very much for your appreciative letter, I'm very
touched, no kidding! I really like working on a project like
that & it's an honour to work for a book of such fine quality.
Paddy is a true poet in that he imparts the essence of poetry
into his prose, gives the reader very clear images evoked – not
described; result, one never tires of rereading so I am going to
thank you for letting me do some of the decorations. I enjoyed
doing them. And, thank you too for the preview – very nice
printing & how well the red binding goes with the dust jacket!

I should like 6 copies if I may at a participant's courtesy
discount but I'll look in sometime & see you if that's easier
for you – best Autumn Greetings
John

Prior to publication, philhellene Harold Nicolson had been full
of praise when he received the *Mani* typescript, writing initially
that he was 'absolutely entranced' because Paddy 'writes like
an angel'. He recommended that Leigh Fermor ought to be
allowed two volumes but by the time he reached the end of
the text he had revised his opinion slightly.

Harold Nicolson to John Murray VI, Neville Terrace, London,
7 July 1955

My Dear Jock

I have now finished the typescript of Paddy's book which
you sent me. I am not quite clear how much more of this

section on the Mani exists. I have a feeling that it would be a good thing if it was brought to an end somewhere about the point where he has now got to, since I fear that to continue the story might be repetitive. If he can have one volume devoted to the Mani and another volume, or volumes, devoted to other areas of Greece that would be far better. I should hate them to crab any of his material, but if he puts it all into one book the thing will become too cumbersome.

I feel myself that his work on Greece is worth an immense amount of trouble on your part since I really do believe it will become a classic. His whole approach to it and his handling of dialogue and personality is fascinating, as there are bits of really magnificent writing such as meeting Anastasia and Antiope, sunset at Kampos, the description of the woman singing a dirge over an English airman, the last supper in the tower, and the descent to Hades.

I attach a short note about some typing errors which I have observed. I do congratulate you most warmly on having got this splendid book.

Yours ever
Harold

Fellow travel writer Freya Stark was also full of praise for *Mani*, but she wisely gave Jock Murray an early indication that his writing and working style was not conducive to tight publishing deadlines.

Freya Stark to John Murray VI, Hydra, Greece, 27 September 1958

Dearest Jock

If ever you came to Idhra you would not only never be surprised at Paddy's delays, but be surprised at ever getting anything out of him at all: one steps out onto a whitewashed stone-flagged terrace, all yellow sun, and blue pearl shadow, with a huge deep triangle of sea and the white houses scattering down to it at all angles round the corner of the town. Two little hills against the sea have cactus and prickly pear up rock sides and a ruined windmill that looks like a watch-tower on top; and on the other side of the house is a hillside of brown terraces and olives, where a goatherd talks to his flocks. There is no car on the island. Apart from the steamer and some frigidaires one is living the classic life and finding it very good.

I am in the middle of Paddy's book and think it first rate. I think he writes better than I do – more consciously and with a fine choice of words. It is just the right length and should have a great success. He gives wonderful descriptions of rock and sky and the gauntness and <u>intensity</u> of this land – I do hope it will be liked as it deserves.

Tomorrow or Monday I go back to Athens (Embassy). It is very exciting to think of finding my book and I suppose it will be out this week or next? If possible, do you think one could hint to some reviewer – possibly TLS – to notice Xenophon in my chapter 15? I am so anxious that my little <u>new</u> discovery should be entered into the stream of Alexander.

Hope for letters soon.

Love

Freya

John Betjeman was another visitor at Paddy and Joan Leigh Fermor's house in Kardamyli. As so often, in his letter he mentions various other members of Jock Murray's circle.

John Betjeman to John Murray VI, 19 September 1969

Dear Jock,

If you can find among all the rubbish written by me, which you have, a broadcast I wrote about Sir Henry Newbolt, would you be so kind as to send it to Patric Dickinson . . . together with any other stuff you possess, which I have written about [Sir Henry] Newbolt. Patrick is writing his life. If it is like Newbolt it will be a very quiet book.

I thought Greece inexpressibly beautiful in its variety of scenery, in its light, and in the siting of the temples, more than the temples themselves, which were too Pevsnerised for me. The Byzantine churches were ravishing, and Osbert [Lancaster]'s book an invaluable guide to them. Osbert has that gift that I've noticed all good artists have, which is that of making one see a place through their eyes. The towns and churches of Greece were just like Osbert's drawings. What I was not prepared for was the splendour of their interiors. At Mistra, Osbert's book was invaluable. It is also full of very funny jokes. What is very badly needed as an accompaniment to Osbert's book is another one on Greek Orthodox rites and ceremonies and mysticism, so that one would know when one went into a Greek church what to do, and how they regard the lighting of candles, and what one should do when one sees an ikon, and what happens at their Masses, in fact the Orthodox outlook on life needs explaining. I took off my hat whenever I saw a vicar, and used to get a blessing, oh, it was interesting.

Paddy [Leigh Fermor]'s house is a masterpiece. Wherever you look there is thought. It is a book, and more lasting than a book can be. It is rather as though Paddy were

Lutyens and Gertrude Jekyll in one designing Greece. The
house is part of the country and Paddy said to me he
wanted a house into whose doors a hen could walk without
looking out of place. It really is a bit of perfection, and he
and Joanie are so happy and kind to the three of us, that I
shall never cease to be grateful.

I dined with the [Stavros] Niarchos's and went on their
yacht, and then I went down with fever in Spetzai. By the
time I reached Paddy and Joan I got a stoppage, which
meant a doctor had to be called over the mountains, and
down that path over the fields in the middle of the night, to
give me an injection against pain. There was talk of my
being moved to hospital at Kalamata, but dread of such a
thing in my subconscious caused me to recover, except for a
violent attack of piles.

Sir Michael Stewart, the ambassador, got George Seferis and
his wife to dinner at the Embassy, the night before last, and
they both sent deep affection to you and Osbert. I can quite
understand Osbert not wanting to go there. I had not realised
that prison in the Balkan countries is accompanied by torture
and beating up, traditionally. Many of George's friends are in
prison, and he is more or less confined to house arrest. He
cannot speak except to people who call at the house with the
milk, and that sort of thing. I got this all from his wife and not
from him. I talked to him only about poetry and how good he
was at writing it. His wife told me that he had offers to live
abroad but preferred to remain in his own country, despite the
inconvenience. I can understand this. His inspiration comes
from the local as does Paddy's, and Paddy has found his home
in Greece. This is a very long letter, I will stop.

Yours

John B.

Though his books on Greece were highly acclaimed, Leigh Fermor's greatest works are widely considered to be his accounts of his youthful walk across Europe in 1933–5. Published in three volumes, they took decades to produce: *A Time of Gifts* (1977), *Between the Woods and the Water* (1986) and *The Broken Road* (2013), posthumously edited by Artemis Cooper and Colin Thubron. This trilogy had begun in 1962 as a commissioned 5,000-word article on 'The Pleasures of Walking', but was expanded and extended over the decades, especially after the chance rediscovery of one of his travel journals.

Patrick Leigh Fermor to John Murray VI, Kardamyli, Greece,
10 January 1973

Dear Jock

I'm so sorry being such an age writing. I knew it would have to be a long-ish letter, so kept putting it off till the decks were a bit clearer of the ludicrous nonsense that has been cluttering till now. I mentioned mysteriously in my last letter a plan I wanted to put to you – I think I told you that when I went down the Danube a few years ago, I went to see my old friend Balasha Cantacuzène (the dedicatee of The Traveller's Tree). When she and her sister were chucked out of their old home in Moldovia by the new regime, they were given a quarter of an hour to pack – a brisk deracination after three centuries – and were then herded off to the west of Wallachia, where they still are (where I went to see them at dead of night). One of the things salvaged was great lumps of my diary (covering the period I've written about in the present book), which I brought back here. The two versions tally pretty well, on the whole, though there are obvious divergences owing to the difference between recalling things that happened thirty-nine years ago — 1934–9 — and scribbling them down on a café table a couple of hours after. The parts covered are: Slovakia and a bit of Hungary; then a long gap, caused by an idle summer loitering from schloss to schloss in Transylvania; then quite a lot of Bulgaria, Bucharest, Bulgaria again (down the Black Sea coast); and Constantinople. The emergence of this long-lost document has been a bit of a curse and a puzzle. It should have cropped up before I started, or when it was too late. What I plan to do is take details out of it to give the text more verifying detail where it is needed. In one or two cases fairly radical changes will have to be made. This is all to the good, as the rewritten first part (which I have dealt with so cursorily in the first version) is now expanded to considerable length, and contains a lot of detail, and this new stuff will give the post-Vienna part a considerable boost, I hope.

My original plan was to finish the book on board the boat sailing to Salonica and Mt Athos, from Constantinople. Now a new idea has begun to sprout.

The diary, after Constantinople, goes on to Mt Athos, in considerable detail, monastery by monastery, covering about a month in mid-winter, ending just after my twentieth birthday. The whole of the diary, I hasten to say, extremely immature, ignorant, awkward, pretentious and inhibited by turns, an odd mixture of pseudo-sophistication and naïveté, and also wittingly and unwittingly comic, often embarrassing. This summer, as a joke and an experiment, I read long passages out loud to people staying here, who insisted on more, so I read the lot. They would agree with all my comments above, but said that nevertheless it had a sort of immediacy and freshness that later reminiscences lack, obviously. So last time I went to Athens, I got someone to type it out, to have a better look; and a rereading suggests this: that I might shorten some of these passages, cut out the awkward or embarrassing bits, and dock the repetitions, but leave the style unchanged, and insert them, here and there, after telling the story of the diary's untimely recovery, as a sort of counterpoint to existing text. It's an odd idea, and presents the difficulty of entire discrepancy of style (because, although I'm the 1934 diarist's descendant, I could also be his grandfather); but, if handled with skill, it might give a sudden new dimension to the book which would be all to the good; and the clash of the two styles might have a special point of its own.

Well that's the first idea. The second is this. After Mt Athos, I went to stay with some people in Macedonia, and the Venizelist revolution broke out, which I managed to accompany on horseback, on a borrowed steed, and attached unofficially to a Royalist cavalry squadron, across Macedonia and Thrace; when it was over, after a week or two, I rode back to the Chalkidiki alone, returned the horse, and continued my uninterrupted walk south, through Macedonia and Thessaly to the Meteora, to Boeotia, through Attica and Athens, where the walk stopped for good, and an entire new life began, which I can't write about – Rumania etc.

I've long been wondering what I should do about this first introduction to Greece, which, after all, has been far more important to me than any of the other countries the book traverses; and now the following solution looms: to prune and cut down drastically, to about an eighth of its present length, the Mt Athos diary; write another chapter on the revolution, and final chapter covering the month it then took me to walk to Athens – possibly ending at the first glimpse of Athens from Eleusis; then writing THE END.

With considerable trepidation, I'm sending you a few
random pages of the central European diary, and the whole
of Mt Athos. Bear all my strictures in mind, I implore!
Whatever else you think about it I can guarantee a few
laughs, however unintended.

No more now, as this has been quite long enough. It's 11
p.m. and pouring with rain, a steady windless downpour –
music to our ears, thinking of all the trees – your plane is
prospering beautifully – and the masses of rosemary hedges
we have been planting.

Yours ever
Paddy

34

'I've been bribed to go on RTE'
Dervla Murphy

————◆————

Bicycling traveller Dervla Murphy's first book, *Full Tilt: Ireland to India with a Bicycle* (1965), was typical of her journeys and writing: full of verve, insight and danger. While in Delhi she met Penelope Betjeman, whose husband John introduced her to Jock Murray. She fitted very well into the long line of Murray's adventurous travel writers and developed a remarkably close and trusting relationship with Jock and Diana Murray, in an age when such personal friendships were becoming increasingly rare in publishing.

A natural and fearless traveller for over half a century, her trips took her to many countries including Ethiopia, Afghanistan, Peru, Laos and Romania. For her books, she adopted a diary style that suited her well and gave her writing an immediacy and a wide appeal. Giving up smoking was always a challenge to her, as was evident when Murphy was completing her account of her eight months travelling in post-communist Transylvania and Romania, published as *Transylvania and Beyond* (1992).

Dervla Murphy to John Murray VI, Old Market, Ireland,
8 January 1991

Dearest Jock

   MOST URGENT!!! Could you please send me a cheque

for £3,500 in exchange for the enclosed – otherwise I may soon end up in prison which would be v. inconvenient before end of Rum. vol. (Irish prisons too overcrowded for work.)

Have decided (today) that it's stupid to try and give up smoking, just cos it's New Year, in the middle of revision. So am back on the weed as from this a.m. but that really is only a postponement – which of course you won't believe till I've proved it! I'll be depending on my Scots blood to see me thro'; it was when I realised that mini-cigars cost me more than £1,000 a year that I resolved to STOP.

Do hope your physio did magical things with the leg. Haven't yet taken mine to my physio but will soon if it doesn't cure itself.

Much love to you both –
D. XX

Although a famous traveller and writer, Murphy has always preferred to keep a low profile and been reluctant to give television or radio interviews. The news in this letter must therefore have come as something of a surprise to those at Albemarle Street.

Dervla Murphy to John Murray VI, Old Market, Ireland,
11 November 1991

Dearest D&J

Work going well on Rum. restructuring (pity not as easy with a country as a book!) and this just to let you know I hope to have completed TS in your sticky paws by 15 Jan. latest and possibly week or so earlier. I'll then appear myself, when you've had time to go over it – week or so later? Let me know eventually if this all sounds OK date-wise for you. Meanwhile the big news is that I've been bribed to go on RTE TV series about authors and their working methods – bribery technique so convoluted I'll have to wait and explain in person! The team arrives on 11 Dec. so keep your fingers crossed for me that day. I enclose bit of nonsense from Cork Examiner which may amuse you – also, oddly enough, about my working methods (being used in this case to pad out!).

Jock, your cheque arrived just now and as you say whatever imbalance either way can be sorted out in due course thro' No. 50 kitty. Mr [Charles] Haughey's★ notion about taxing money in deposit accounts must have driven an awful lot of cash out of Ireland! Thank you for coming to the rescue. Lots of love to both.

In haste – D. XX

★ To no one's surprise, he has survived yet again.

P.T.O. Thanks too for excellent review of Garnett's auto-biog. & V.G. article on Rum.

The circumstances of the 'bribery technique' were afterwards explained in the following letter, which also mentions her attendance at the International Festival of Authors in Harbourfront, Toronto, Canada.

Dervla Murphy to John Murray VI, Old Market, Ireland, Monday, 25 November 1991

Dearest Jock

A letter to be treasured – yours of Sat. 16 Nov. I only collect my post on Mondays, to keep that source of distraction to the minimum. So didn't read it till today.

Points raised: I'll deal with them in an orderly fashion, as they come.

a) Harbourfront financial arrangements were all expenses paid (except getting from Ireland to Gatwick, which seemed to slip between the cracks), plus Can. $500.

b) Baffled by your ref. to 'grand invitation' – <u>what</u> invitation? Please elucidate!

c) Krisna – completely agree with you; he made sense only on education – but a lot there.

d) Nasty agent at Harbourfront – I've no idea who he was: they swarmed, and unlike us authors didn't have to wear name-tags. He was youngish, tallish, fattish, dark-haired, smooth talker, dressed to kill, <u>slight</u> Welsh accent, tended to ignore all the as yet unknown names and hover around Doris Lessing, Newby, Holroyd et al – which I thought a bit short-sighted, given wealth of commercially unexploited talent all around us.

e) Sorry didn't enclose <u>Cork Examiner</u>; now can't find – prob'ly lit fire with it.

f) Irish income tax: we have to pay on the deposit itself, not merely on the interest on it, one of Haughey's less popular devices. Incidentally, the inevitable, I believe, has happened and cos of EEC 'harmonization' of taxation our 'artist's exemption' from income tax will soon be ended.

g) 11 Dec. TV ordeal – funny genesis – friend of mine took a bet with a friend of hers who works in Telefis Eireann that she (my friend) could persuade me to go on the box. RTE person said <u>no way</u> could anyone get me on the box so the bet was for £300. And my friend is destitute at the moment cos husband recently absconded (vanished without a trace) leaving her with three small children – so I could hardly refuse to earn £300 for her by saying 'Yes' to this chap whose name I can't remember. It's apparently a series about writer's working methods, etc. However, this story is <u>not</u> to be publicized please!

h) Alas! I didn't read the Annual Report of the Green Alliance so we may deduce that if I had it wouldn't have stimulated me. A very ungreen waste of paper – or would be if not put to good use by ecologically sound folk such as your correspondent.

i) Good but unsurprising news that Paddy on best-seller list (tho' I sometimes wonder nowadays quite what that signifies). I'll bet you enjoyed romping around the country with him! I'm much looking forward to reading the vol. – meant to ask you to ask him to sign one for me but forgot till he'd left.

j) Wouldn't have thought you needed a handsome American female psychologist to prove Byron a manic-depressive – surely his letters proof enough!

k) I last went to church about 43 years ago – not counting the hatching, matching and dispatching social occasions. Or the anthropologically inspired visits to services in Belfast, Ethiopia or Rumania. I 'go to church', in the sense of communicating with Something Else Out There, when I'm walking or cycling <u>alone</u> in the mountains – we all have our little peculiarities. Tho' actually that's quite a common one.

The only O[ld] M[arket] news is sad. Eilish not making progress, tho' the 5-hour op. to remove abscess from aorta and replace four valves went well – heart now fine. I've just rung Brian and conveyed your message of thoughts and prayers, which was <u>much</u> appreciated. It seems to be one of these cases that totally baffle doctors. Poor B. is working hard at the stiff-upper-lip but by now beginning to show the strain – it's been going on for 3½ months. Cancer ruled out completely, which is in a way disconcerting; you can or can't <u>do</u> something about cancer. This debilitating mysterious infection, being unsuccessfully treated with a combination of antibiotics in drip form, is a nightmare. I'm going to Dublin tomorrow to see E. briefly – she's not equal to having even B. around for v. long – and spend a couple of nights with B. to cheer him up (I hope!) cos he's all alone in the big house. He'll be 80 next April – hard to believe! Apart from when under stress, as now, he gives the impression of being about 65.

Thank you for the cuttings; both riveting. Wonder why David Spark didn't mention that the unaffected village was

more than 3,000 feet <u>above</u> Nyos – the one we passed
through before our swim. Orthodox article v. thought-
provoking; I could write pages on it but won't – at least not
yet! So little news about Rum. in media, but I hear from
friends that things v. grim in the cities this winter; extreme
shortages of food, light and heat, almost as in the pre-coup
times. That's in Bucharest and Iasi; I expect E'ma mail will
bring more news from Cluj etc. <u>BEESWAX</u> – Hope you
approve of the change of title . . . and Beyond seems essential when quite a bit about Moldavia and something about
Bucharest. I reckon <u>Transylvania and Beyond</u> OK cos gives
sense of movement. I'm sure John is right about a fresh eye;
this book seems to have been haunting the three of us for
decades and we're probably past seeing it straight. I've been
very obedient and kept to the 15,000 you allocated for final
chapters. Through pruning and removing Historical Intro.
(replaced by Chronology) I think we now have a version not
much longer but a great deal better than the original.
Bibliography not needed. All other bits and pieces are
enclosed. The map will be important. I fancy the Bicaz Pass
photo I sent you for jacket.

I'll ring tomorrow evening to check that TS has arrived.

Further details of the interview were revealed in a subsequent
letter.

*Dervla Murphy to John Murray VI, Old Market, Ireland,
12 December 1991*

Dearest D&J

Just to let you know I've survived yesterday's TV ordeal.
David Hanley is someone special, not at all one's image of a

Famous TV Personality. He arrived at O. M. 12.30 p.m. and he and I went off to a pub and discovered how much we had in common and sank three pints of Guinness each while the crew were turning my workroom into a TV studio. By the time we returned at 2.0 p.m. I was so drunk (3 pints in 90 mins is like an athlete being given steroids – especially as I've been on the waggon while working) I couldn't care less about cameras, the viewing public or anything else. So I just nattered on incoherently for the required 28 mins after which David and I returned to the pub for more pints (number forgotten) whilst the crew dismantled everything. David said he'd let me know when the programme will be shown; I explained I'd no desire to see it but asked him to send you the tape (or is it called a video now?) cos I thought you might be amused to see a drunken author on camera.

Radio 4 tells me you are having appalling weather but here it's one of the most pleasant mid-winters I can remember: no rain, frost, wind, snow – perfect cycling weather. Today went for 30 miles on the tight little network of roads around the Knockmealdowns – met only <u>one</u> car. Magical mid-winter silence and stillness. Grey sky but not low cloud so the dimly blue mountains ever-present. Then around noon little sunshine filtered thro' and all the shades of gorse and bracken and heather and grass showed in that strange subdued mid-winter way – matched by the birdsong, also subdued but constant. Sometimes I wonder why I ever leave Ireland; starting from West Waterford, one certainly isn't travelling in search of beauty. Maybe I should make John happy by forgetting my Mystery Tour and pedalling around the 32 counties! But actually that project will benefit from being embarked on immediately after the relaxing Mystery

Tour. Then I'll be both a native and someone who has been for X months completely cut off from events – so a native exploring. The pace of change is so extraordinary everywhere – even in Ireland! – that after a longish absence there will be a lot to explore on home territory.

Lismore's elevation to being one of Ireland's twelve 'Heritage Towns' (EEC-funded) has been getting me into trouble. At first the local organizers optimistically assumed they could wheel me on as a 'local resource' – i.e., include in their brochure Famous Author who would sign books for fans on Tues. and Thur. from May to Sept.!!! You can imagine the four-letter words with which the Famous Author dismissed that ploy; by C[annon] L[odge] law, the fines would have been about £5. Next I was asked to submit to the Dublin fund – controllers suggested visual improvements around Lismore. That of course inspired a passionate and lengthy document – followed by quasi-political complications. By sheer coincidence – <u>no</u> collusion – my thoughts about Lismore as a Heritage Town happen to be identical to Paul's, of which the locals do not approve. So not only have I refused to be a 'resource', I'm also making all the wrong noises on 'development'. It's all an interesting illustration of the hang-ups persisting (and new ones being acquired) in 1990s. In fact, the episode would make quite a good beginning to the Irish vol.!

Lots of special C'mas love (tied with a red bow) and may you have a very happy '92.

Dervla xx

Jock and his wife Diana worked closely with Dervla on editing and preparing her books for publication, the success of this partnership owing much to the deep trust and understanding between them. When she visited London a visit to Murray's was always the highlight.

Dervla Murphy to John Murray VII, Old Market,
1 December 1992

World Aids Day

My Dear John

This is a mere embryo, the typescript [the first draft of *The Ukimwi Road*] unread by me so all typing as well as other errors in place – don't bother doing anything about the former. I reckon there are about 75,000 here – post-pruning, probably 60,000-ish. Repetitions are deliberate; when revising/rewriting I decide where's best to deal with what, if you follow me. Another four chapters to come, I think shorter than these certainly (you'll be relieved to hear!) less AIDS and more action. You won't find this a cheering read; it wasn't a cheering journey and it isn't cheering to write about. But that's life in Africa now; to be cheerful you need to be blind and deaf.

Ruthless criticism expected/needed – who wants a pussy-footing editor?! Not me. When you're trying to flog the book you can pretend it's wonderful; at this stage you must admit it's a load of garbage – and say why in words of one syllable and possibly four letters. What a life we lead! Who'd be a publisher or an author given a choice? But Fate deprives some people of choice and one has to knuckle under one's destiny . . .

Hope the improvement continuing with Cannon Lodge – I much look forward to seeing them both but Diana must

say if for any reason when it comes to the time it's easier if
I don't stay — I can always doss down with the Cecils who
are within walking distance of C. L. Great rejoicing among
the Irish — or at least those of them who want their country
to begin to grow up — because that is what the general election results indicate is happening . . . Very amused by the
BBC's slip-up on reporting on abortion referenda results —
they don't often get the facts wrong, but in bulletin after
bulletin they reported: 'The Irish Republic has again voted
to reject legal abortion' — situation obviously too compli-
cated for any non-Irish observer to grasp! Happily the NO
vote on the abortion clause and the YES votes on the other
two clauses means the Irish have voted YES to abortion, tho'
in a very subtle and convoluted way.

P.T.O. for odd Penguin mistake about Paddy's Peru —
saying it was first published in the '70s! There's more and
more carelessness of this sort around — good old-fashioned
standards all shot to pieces!

STOP PRESS! Have just been on to my travel agent and
there is a slight change of date — I'll be arriving London late
on evening of Sunday 13 Dec., spending following night
14th at C. L. if that is still on, leaving Stansted 9.15 a.m. Wed.
16. And the BBC thing is 2.30 p.m. 15th, so when do you
suggest we get together re: TS? This change is cos the C'mas
fares start on the 17th! The ticket I'm getting is only £58
return! Pretty good.

35

'The VERY BEST publishers'
In Praise of John Murray

———◆———

Murray's often received complaints: over a perceived lack of attention to a literary manuscript or to replying to correspondence, or over a sense of injustice with sales, a book's expenses or share of profits; sometimes misunderstandings or clashes of personality arose. John Murray II in 1805, when arbitrating between two feuding publishers, cautioned them against over-hasty correspondence: 'Recollect how serious every dispute becomes upon paper, where a man writes a thousand asperities merely to show or support his superior ability. Things that would not have been spoken, or perhaps even thought of, in conversation, are stated and horribly magnified upon paper.'

Authors irritated by delays in communication or in publishing their books often vented their frustrations by letter. Many were exasperated by John Murray II's negligent attitude to correspondence. Thomas Moore wrote to poet Mary Anne Cursham on 19 June 1828: 'He is notorious for not deigning to answer anyone, from poets down to peers.' Poet and writer Allan Cunningham had proposed some new works to Murray on 10 March 1837, writing again on 25 March that 'I would prefer the name of Murray for a book of mine to any other.' The continued lack of a reply prompted this frustrated, but amusing, follow-up.

Allan Cunningham to John Murray II, Lower Belgrave Place, London, 21 April 1837

Sleepest thou or wakest thou, O John Murray: thou art foremost of the honourable and the generous of the ancient tribe of publishers; yet verily thou art a sloth in motion, a snail in correspondence and the most dilatory of all Conservatives.

Enoch was thy ancestor for he took twenty-seven years to answer his first love letter; that Irish hero was thy relative who had to be awakened with a stick or a stone: one of the Seven Sleepers had his roost high in the tree of thy genealogy, and thou art more than cousin to that drowsiest of all diplomatists Lord Glenelg who has slept through the noisiest administration since the first parliament of Babel. Still your cry is, leave me leave me to repose: to repose I shall assuredly leave you if you will but say either Yes or No to the communication which I made to you some month or so ago.

Yours always
Allan Cunningham

Luckily for the Murrays the numerous letters of complaint and abuse were interspersed with genuine letters of admiration and appreciation of their friendship. Explorer Paul Du Chaillu had several successful books with Murray's as well as ones that were less so. However, he felt such loyalty and attachment to the Murrays that he always valued their association, regardless of his publishing position or location.

Paul Belloni Du Chaillu to John Murray III, New York,
17 March 1871

> Annotated by one of the Murrays:
> 'friendly letter'.

My Dear Friend Murray

Cooke and I thought I would write to you also. I can
assure you that I have thought of you many and many a
time since I have left London and that I have talked of you
to my friends and of the very pleasant time I had often had
at your house. Of course everybody who is not a donkey
knows the name of John Murray here, for your father and
your publications have gone all over the world where the
English language is spoken. You do not know how much I
look forward to the time when we meet again, and this is
going to take place sometime next May, so do not be astonished if a fine morning you see your friend Paul Du Chaillu
make his humble appearance before his London publisher
and friend.

I am sure I will receive a hearty greeting from you and
from your family. I am as much of a boy as I ever was and
very fond of a play. But I suppose all the Murrays are now
either young ladies and young gentlemen, no more children.
It makes me feel old when I think of that; the likeness I
send you will show you that my hair on the top of my head
has not increased in thickness. I can't help it.

If it was not an account of a new book I have on hand
and which I want to finish entirely before I said I would be
in England before May, but now I have got into a habit of
printing a book a year for the juveniles. I would like to
remain long in England but I have to go to Norway and

Sweden and I must be back in New York in November, but I could not go to Europe without taking a look at old England, so I will stop to see the old friends of whom I have kept so very many pleasant recollections.

I am sorry to hear that our good friend Sir Roderick Murchison has been so ill. I am glad he is better. I hope I will be able to see him.

Now, my dear Murray, do not follow my example; write to me, I promise to answer you <u>at once</u>.

Please give my kindest remembrance to Mrs Murray, to the <u>children,</u> and to our mutual friends, and with kindest regards

Believe me

Your very sincere friend

P. B. Du Chaillu

Josiah Whymper was one of the great engravers of the nineteenth century, a profession followed by his son Edward, who also became one of the leading mountaineers and travel writers of his generation. The family association with Murray's was strong, as recognised in this letter.

Edward Whymper to John Murray IV, 13 June 1904

Dear Mr Murray

I am glad to hear that you will accept the copyright of Scrambles and of Andes, and the stock which may remain in your possession at the time of my death. The proposition was made to you without due consideration, and I think that my interest will be better served by this arrangement than by any other that I could make.

I have directed my confidential clerk, Mr Frank Aylett, to prepare the illustrations for delivery to you, and in the event of my non-return from Canada he is instructed to deliver them to you at once. I propose to return from Canada at the end of August, and, if I can do so, will bring them to Albemarle Street myself.

I have now had experience of your house for a clear fifty years, and whether as errand boy, draughtsman, engraver, printer, or author, my experiences have been satisfactory. The connection of my father with your house goes back at least twenty-five years more. I have heard him say, several times, that, although the amount of business done was unimportant, he had more pleasure in dealing with you than with any other house with which he was associated. I say the same.

Faithfully yours
Edward Whymper

The American writer Washington Irving was read throughout the world and became a literary icon in his homeland, as well as in Britain and Spain. One of his compatriots, otherwise unknown despite sharing a famous name, sent this letter of thanks and appreciation to Murray.

Francis Bacon to John Murray IV, Nutholme, Ridgefield, Connecticut, USA, 25 June 1907

My Dear Mr Murray

Among the pleasant recollections of our recent stay in London, none have left a more agreeable impression than our visit to 50 Albemarle St and our hospitable reception there.

My mother was an English woman, and a great admirer of Washington Irving and particularly his Sketch Book, and long before I became connected with the Irving family I appreciated her admiration for the distinguished author.

I have recently re-read the Sketch Book, and where can be found a more charming description of Westminster Abbey, the most noble and interesting edifice to be found on either hemisphere? I was particularly struck with Irving's tribute to your grandfather, the founder of your house, to whom with Sir Walter Scott he always felt he was much indebted for the success of his literary work. He says, 'From that time Murray became my publisher, conducting himself in all his dealings with that fair, open and liberal spirit which obtained for him the well merited appellation the "Prince of Book Sellers".' No wonder at the success of the Murrays, and what a pleasure it must be to you to be able to continue the name and reputation of so worthy and distinguished a founder. Long may the name and the firm continue.

Mrs Bacon desires to unite with me in our kind remembrances to Mrs Murray and yourself, and I hope you will remember that if you are ever in New York, it will give us great pleasure to see you there.

Faithfully yours
Francis M. Bacon

The friendship between Harold Nicolson, a distinguished diplomat, critic and writer, and John Murray VI was cemented over their mutual love of Lord Byron, whose archives Jock Murray cared for so well. Nonetheless, it required all Murray's resources of diplomacy to raise the issue of Harold's personal hygiene.

Harold Nicolson to John Murray VI, Neville Terrace, London,
11 April 1946

Dear Jock

I consider that it is of the utmost delicacy on your part
to have sent me a cake of soap. Gratitude goes well with
cleanliness, and as you have given me both I thank you for
each.

Yours ever, my dear Jock

Harold

While friendships are often formed at university, in the case of
John Murray VI and John Betjeman it proved to be not only
an enduring bond, but also a remarkably successful publishing
collaboration, starting with *Continual Dew* (1937), through two
and a half million copies of his *Collected Poems* (1958), his verse
autobiography *Summoned by Bells* (1960) to *Betjeman's Cornwall*
(1984) in his last year. This charming letter was typical of their
decades of friendship.

John Betjeman to John Murray VI, 28 January 1976

Dear Jock

Very many thanks for the quarter bottles of bubbly and
Guinness. They are essential to the winter mornings. You are
the kindest of publishers, the truest of friends and the
worthiest communicant in the parish of Hampstead. I can
come and see you any time on Tuesday February 3rd, the
later the better, i.e. 4.30.

Yours ever

John B.

Illustrator Beryl Cook's delightfully comical pictures of burly and burlesque British characters were reproduced in posters, postcards and many books by a number of publishers, including Murray's. She was therefore well placed to appreciate the value of being published by Murray's.

Beryl Cook, née Lansley, to John Murray VI, 27 April 1980

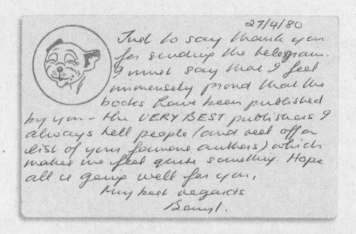

Just to say thank you for sending the telegram. I must say that I feel immensely proud that the books have been published by you – the VERY BEST publishers I always tell people (and reel off a list of your famous authors) which makes me feel quite something. Hope all is going well for you,

My best regards
Beryl

ACKNOWLEDGEMENTS

There are many acknowledgements and thanks that it is my pleasure to give, from the conception to the publication of this book. First in thanks, in this and so much else, are John and Virginia Murray, as well as the wider Murray family. They are the embodiment and perfection of all that is admirable about Murray's. My only hope for this book is that they feel it to be in some measure a fair reflection of the remarkable history of John Murray's traditions and archives, of which they have both been true custodians.

Thanks to their generosity and foresight the incomparable John Murray Archive was entrusted to the National Library of Scotland. Ten years of curating it leaves too many colleagues, academics and friends to name individually, but thanks are due to them all. Some former colleagues deserve additional recognition, however, including Martyn Wade and Dr John Scally, the former and current National Librarians, as well as Kirsty McHugh, my successor as curator of the John Murray Archive. Special thanks are also due to my closest colleagues: Rachel Beattie and Helen Symington.

The best traditions of the publishing house of Murray have continued. While managing director of John Murray (Publishers), Roland Philipps first conceived of this work, and Nick Davies, his successor, has been an enthusiastic supporter throughout.

Caroline Westmore has worked tirelessly and sympathetically in editing the work and proved invaluable in her advice on the selection of letters. My appreciation is also due to the rest of the Murray team: Rosie Gailer and Alice Herbert for publicity, Morag Lyall for sympathetic copy-editing, Howard Davies for proofreading, Jon Gray and Sara Marafini for the cover art and Rachel Southey for production. An extra note of thanks is also due to Professor Dr Agustín Coletes Blanco for his assistance in transcribing a particularly troublesome letter, and the gracious scholar Tom Bean for corrections and amendments.

The best advice and support is often imparted by friends, especially over a beer, for which take a bow Mark Mulhern. Without a loving and encouraging family who can achieve anything? Heartfelt thanks, then, to my parents Jim and Mar-Lee, my wife Anna and our son Alexander.

Edinburgh, June 2018

SOURCES AND CREDITS

The majority of letters are either in the John Murray Collection, London, or the John Murray Archive at the National Library of Scotland, Edinburgh. The NLS reference numbers are: Arnot Ms.40026; Austen Ms.42001; Bacon Ms.40035; Baedeker Ms.42613; Barry Ms.40063; Benson Ms.40086; Bird Ms.42027; Blackwood Ms.40114; Borrow Ms.42041; Burnes Ms.42048; Byron (1813) Ms.43487, (1814) Ms.43488, (1819) Ms.43490; Callcott Ms.40185; Campbell Ms.42052; Carlyle Ms.42058; Chaillu Ms.40206; Clowes Ms.41280; Cook Ms. 42613; Croker Ms.42129; Cunningham Ms.40300; Darwin (1859) Ms.42153, (1860) Ms.42152; D'israeli Ms.42160; Disraeli Ms.42625; Eastlake Ms.42174; Edwards Ms.40367; Elwin (1854) Ms. 42192, (1859) Ms.42197, (1865) Ms.42199, (1871) Ms.42200, (1875, 1878) Ms.42201; Finden Ms.40402; Ford Ms.42224; Gifford Ms.42248; Gibbs–Smith Ms.41103; Gladstone Ms.42260; Graham Ms.40185; Hogg Ms.42305; Hooker Ms.40573; Hopkins Ms.40577; Irving Ms.42308; 'John Bull' Ms.40167; Kent Acc.12927/H8; Kinglake Ms.40651; Lamb Ms.43456 (forgery), Ms.43467; Livingstone Ms.42420; Livingstone Film Expedition Acc.12927/324; Lockhart Gibson Ms.42445; MacRae Acc.12927/382; Mahon Ms.41145; Melville Ms.42477; Mendelssohn Ms.42613; Milman Ms.40820; Milton Ms.40828; Moore Ms.42486; Munthe Acc.12927/382; Murray III Ms.43059; Norton Ms.42507; Palgrave Ms.40902; Peel Ms.42517; Philomath Ms.42308; Rundell Ms.41046; Scott (1816) Ms.42540,

John Murray Esq.
Fleet Street
London

TUNBRIDGE-WELLS A SP 16 72
Immediate and confidential
John Murray Esq.
50 Albemarle Street
London W.
ROMA (FERROVIA)
Inghilterra
50 Albemarle St. London
Himself alone: Urgent
Sir John Murray, K.C.V.O., D.S.O.
Publisher Royal,
50, Albemarle Street,
London, W.1.

BY AIR MAIL
PAR AVION

Messrs John Murray Ltd,

50 Albemarle St,

London. W.1.

ENGLAND.

PAR AVION

Taranaki
New Zealand

The Vetting Ogre
Murray, John (Publishers) Ltd
50 Albemarle Street
LONDON
England
W1X 4BD

NEW ZEALAND

New Zealand

Printed Papers Reduced Rate

JOHN MURRAY'S LIST

If not delivered please return to
50 Albemarle St., London, W.1

RETOUR

London W. 1
(UK)

NATIONAL BANK BUILDING,
PAKISTAN

From Byron, Austen and Darwin

to some of the most acclaimed and original
contemporary writing, John Murray takes pride in
bringing you powerful, prizewinning, absorbing
and provocative books that will entertain you
today and become the classics of tomorrow.

We put a lot of time and passion into what we
publish and how we publish it, and we'd like to
hear what you think.

Be part of John Murray – share your views with us at:

www.johnmurray.co.uk

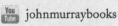 johnmurraybooks

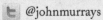 @johnmurrays

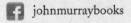 johnmurraybooks